MW01709466

Aión: Aiónios

John Wesley Hanson

Printed in the United States of America

ISBN:1631741209

PREFACE

The verbal pivot on which swings the question, Does the Bible teach the doctrine of Endless Punishment? Is the word *Aión* and its derivatives and reduplications. The author of this treatise has endeavored to put within brief compass the essential facts pertaining to the history and use of the word, and he thinks he has conclusively shown that it affords no support whatever to the erroneous doctrine. It will generally be conceded that the tenet referred to is not contained in the Scriptures if the meaning of endless duration does not reside in the controverted word. The reader is implored to examine the evidence presented, as the author trusts it has been collected, with a sincere desire to learn the truth.

AIÓN -- AIÓNIOS

INTRODUCTION

It is a prevalent idea that the words "*Eternal, Everlasting, Forever,*" etc., in the English Bible, signify endless duration. This essay aims to prove the popular impression erroneous. The inquiry will be pursued in a manner that shall be satisfactory to the scholar, and also enable the ordinary reader to apprehend the facts, so that both the learned and the unlearned may be able to see the subject in a light that shall relieve the Scriptures of seeming to teach a doctrine that blackens the character of God, and plunges a deadly sting into the believing heart.

The original Hebrew Bible was translated into Greek, by seventy scholars, and hence called "The Septuagint," B.C. 200-300,(1) and the Hebrew word *Olam* is, in almost all cases, translated *AiónAiónios* etc., (*Aíwv, Aíwvios,*) so that the two words may be regarded as synonymous with each other. In the New Testament the same words*Aión* and its derivatives, are the original Greek of the English words,*Eternal, Everlasting, Forever, etc.*. So that when we ascertain the real meaning of *Aión*, we have settled the sense of those English words in which the doctrine of Endless Punishment is erroneously taught. It is not going to far to say that if the Greek *Aión - Aiónios* does not denote endless duration, then endless punishment is not taught in the

Bible. We proceed to show that the sense of interminable duration does not reside in the word.

Three avenues are open to us in which to pursue this important investigation. I. *Etymology*, II. *Lexicography*, III. *Usage.*

Our first appeal will be to Etymology.

I. ETYMOLOGY

We are aware that nothing is more unsafe and treacherous than the guidance of etymology. An ounce of *usage* is worth a pound of it. Etymology is theory, usage is fact. For instance, our common word prevent is compounded of *præ* and *venio*, to come or go before, and once it had that meaning, but it has long since lost it in common usage, in which it now means to hinder. Suppose two thousand years hence some one should endeavor to prove that in the year 1875 the word prevent meant to go before. He could establish his position by the etymology of the word, but he would be wholly wrong, as would appear by universal usage in our current literature. So that if we agree that the etymology of *Aión* indicates eternity to have been its original meaning, it by no means follows that it had that force in Greek literature. But its derivation does not point in that direction.

LENNEP[(2)]

Says that it comes from *Aó* (to breathe) which suggests the idea of indefinite duration. He says: It was transferred from breathing to collection, or multitude of times. From which proper signification again have been produced those by which the ancients have described either age *(ævum)*, or eternity *(æternitatem,)* or the age of man *(hominis ætatem.)* Commenting on Lennep's derivation of the word, Rev. E. S. Goodwin, says:[(3)] "It would signify a multitude of periods or times united to each other, duration indefinitely continued. Its proper force, in reference to duration, seems to be more that of uninterrupted duration than otherwise; a term of which the duration is continuous as long as it lasts, but which may be completed and finished, as age, dispensation, sæculum, in a general sense.' Mr. Goodwin entertained the theory that the word is from the verb *aió*, its active participle converted into a substantive.

ARISTOTLE'S ETYMOLOGY.

But this etymology is not the popular one. Aristotle,[(4)] the great Greek Philosopher, explained the derivation as a combination of two Greek words *(aei ón)* which signify *always existing.* As there is a great deal of controversy on this famous passage, we will give

THREE TRANSLATIONS OF ARISTOTLE.

I. Dr. Pond[(5)]: In describing the highest heaven, the residence of the gods, Aristotle says: "It is therefore evident that there is neither space, nor time, nor vacuum beyond. Wherefore the things there are not adapted by nature to exist in place; nor does time make them grow old; neither under the highest (heaven) is there any change of any one of these things, they being placed beyond it; but unchangeable, passionless - they continue through all *aióna (eternity.)* For indeed, the word itself *according to the ancients,* divinely expressed this. For the period which comprehends the time of every one's life, beyond which, according to nature, nothing exists, is called his *aión, (eternity.)* And for the same reason, the period of the whole heaven even *the infinite time of all things,* and *the period comprehending that infinity* is *aión, eternity,* deriving its name from *aei, einai, always being,* immortal and divine."

Dr. J. R. Boise,[(6)] Professor of Greek in the University of Chicago: "Time is a notation of motion; and motion without a physical body is impossible. But, beyond the heaven, it has been shown that there is neither a body, nor can there be. It is plain, therefore, that there is neither space, nor void, nor time beyond. Therefore, the things there are not by nature in space, nor does time make them grow old, nor is there any change in any one of those things placed beyond the outermost sweep (or current); but, unchangeable and without passion, having the best and most sufficient life, they continue through all eternity *(aión)*; for this name (i.e., *aión)* has been divinely uttered by the ancients. For the definite period *(to telos),* which embraces the time of the life of each individual, to whom, according to nature, there can be nothing beyond, has been called each ones's eternity *(aión).* And, by parity of reasoning, the definite period also of the entire heaven, even the definite period embracing the infinite time of all things and infinity, is an eternity *(aión),* immortal and divine, having received the appellation (eternity, *aión)* from the fact that it exists always *(apo tou aei einai).*

Dr. Edward Beecher:(7) "The limit of the whole heaven, and the limit enclosing the universal system, is the divine and immortal existing *(aei ón)* (God) deriving his name*Aión* from his ever existing *(aei ón.)*" Dr. B. adds: "From the time of Homer to Plato and Aristotle, about five centuries, the word *aión* is used by poets and historians alongside of various compounds of *aei*, for the compounds of *aei* retain the diphthong *ei*, but *aión* drops the *e*. There is a verb *aió* - to breathe, to live. The passage of Aristotle in which his etymology occurs, *has been mistranslated, for it does not give the etymology of the abstract idea eternity*, but of the concrete idea God, as an ever-existing person, from whom all other personal beings derived existence and life. What Aristotle has been supposed to assert of *aión*, in the sense of eternity, he asserts of *aión* in the sense of God, a living and divine person. That the word *aión* in the classic Greek sometimes denotes God is distinctly stated in Henry Stephens' great lexicon, (Paris edition,) and the passage referred to in Sophocles (Herac. 900,) fully authorized his statement. In that passage Jupiter is called '*Aión*, (the living God) the Son of Kronos.' Moreover, the whole context of Aristotle proves that he is speaking of the great immovable first mover of the universe, the *Aión*, immortal and divine" * * *

This passage from Aristotle is obscure, and if he were authority, it would not settle the question of the meaning of the word. If we adopt this theory, we may claim that *aión* had the primary meaning of *continuous existence*, such being the signification of *aei* and *ón*, but there is no warrant even in such an origin for ascribing to it duration without end. But Aristotle does not say or intimate that the word had the meaning of eternity in his day, nor does his statement of its derivation prove that it had that meaning then. On the contrary, Aristotle's use of the word, as we shall hereafter show, clearly proves that it had no such meaning in his mind, even if it is compounded of*aei* and *ón*.

AEI

The word *aei* from which *aión* is claimed to grow, is found eight times, (perhaps more, though I have not found it oftener) in the New Testament, and in no one instance does it mean endless. Mark xv:8; Acts vii:51; 2Cor. iv:11; vi:10, Titus, i:12; Heb. iii:10; 1Pet. iii:15; 2Pet. i:12. I give two instances. The multitude desired Pilate to release a prisoner, Mark xv:8: "as he had *ever* done with them." Heb. iii:10: "They do *always* err in their heart." An endless duration growing out of a word used thus, would be a curiosity. It is alway, or always, or ever, in each text. Liddell and Scott give more than fifty compounds of *aei*.

Concerning Aristotle's use of the word in his famous sentence, "Life, an *aión* continuous and eternal," it is enough to say that if *aión* intrinsically meant endless, Aristotle never would have sought to strengthen the meaning by adding "continuous" and "eternal," any more than one would say, God has an eternity, continuous and endless. He has a life, an existence, an *aión* endless, just as man's *aión* on earth is limited; just as Idumea's smoke in the Old Testament is *aiónios*. Nor, had Aristotle considered *aión* to mean eternity, would he have said in this very passage: "the time of the life of each individual has been called his *aión*."

Cremer, Liddel and Scott, Donnegan, and Henry Stephens adopt the Aristotleian origin of the word. Grimm rejects it, and Robinson in his latest editions gives both etymologies without deciding between them. Stephens says: "Aristotle, and after him many other philosophers, as Plotinus and Proclus, introduced the etymology of *aión* from *aei*, and thus *added* the idea of eternity to the word."

But we have shown that the famous passage in Aristotle refers to God, *(apo tou aei einai)* and not to abstract duration. We have shown that *aei* is used eight times in the New Testament, and not in the sense of endless, once. We shall prove that Aristotle himself uniformly used the word in the sense of limited duration, and under the head of Classic Usage will hereafter prove that at the time the Old Testament was rendered into Greek, this was the only meaning the word had with any Greek writer. If *aeión*, is its origin, which is more than doubtful, it cannot mean more than continuous existence, the precise length to be determined by accompanying words. Adopt either derivation, and indefinite duration is the easy and natural meaning of the word, if we suffer ourselves to be guided by its etymology. Eternity can only be expressed by it when it is accompanied by other words, denoting endless duration, or by the name of Deity.

All will agree that words may change their meaning, and therefore that etymology is an uncertain guide. If etymology point in one direction, and usage in another, the former must yield; but if both utter one fact, each reinforces and strengthens the other. This we have illustrated by the etymology of 'prevent.' Hundreds of words teach the same truth. Words start out with a certain meaning, and change it in process of time. If *aión* really meant eternity when it was first pronounced, it would not follow that it has this meaning now. That it had not that meaning at first would not hinder it from being thus used subsequently. Etymology proves nothing one way or the other, its evidence is but *prima facie;* usage is the only decisive authority. But etymology gives no warrant for applying the idea of eternity to the word.

THE PLATONIC DERIVATIONS.

We have proceeded on the ground that Aristotle's etymology is authoritative. But nothing is further from the truth. The scholarship of to-day, possessed by an average educated philologist, is far more competent to trace this or any Greek word to its real source, than Plato or Aristotle was able to do. In his analysis of Plato's Cratylus,[(8)] Grote accurately observes of Plato's etymologies: "Though sometimes reasonable enough, they are in a far greater number of instances forced, arbitrary, and fanciful. The transitions of meaning imagined, and the structural transformations of words, are alike strange and violent. Such is the light in which these Platonic etymologies appear to a modern critic. But such was not the light in which they appeared either to the ancient Platonists or critics earlier than the last century. The Platonists even thought then full of mysterious and recondite wisdom. So complete has been the revolution of opinion that the Platonic etymologies are*now* treated by most critics as too absurd to have been seriously intended by Plato, even as conjectures. It is called 'a valuable discovery of modern times' (so Schleiermacher terms it) that Plato meant most of them as mere parody and caricature."

The character of Aristotle as an etymologist is thus stated by Grote: "Nor are they more absurd than many of the etymologies proposed by Aristotle." A slender hook this, whereon to hang such a doctrine as that of the immortal wo of countless millions of souls.

CONCLUSIONS.

The conclusions to which any judicial mind must arrive are these: 1, It is uncertain from what source the word *Aión* sprang; 2, It is of no consequence how it originated; 3, Aristotle's opinion is not authority; and 4, It is probable that he was not defining the word, but was alluding to that being whose *aión*, or existence is continuous and eternal. That he did not understand that *aión* signified eternity, we shall demonstrate from his uniform use of the word, in the sense of limited duration. And we find no reason in its etymology for giving it the sense of endless duration. And if it did thus originate, it does not afford a particle of proof that it was subsequently used with that meaning.

II. LEXICOGRAPHY AND THE CRITICS.

We next appeal to *Lexicography*. Now lexicograph must always be consulted, especially on disputed words, *cum grano salis*. A theologian, in his definitions, is quite certain to shade technical words with his own belief, and lean one way or the other, according to his own predilections. Unconsciously and necessarily the lexicographer who has a bias in favor of any doctrine will tincture his definitions with his own idiosyncracies. Very few have sat judicially, and given meanings to words with reference to their exact usage; so that one must examine dictionaries concerning any word whose meaning is disputed, with the same care that should be used in reference to any subject on which men differ.

With this thought in mind let us consult such of the lexicons as have fallen under our notice, and also some of the Biblical critics who have explored the word.

AUTHORITIES.

The oldest lexicographer, *Hesychius*, (A. D. 400-600,) defines*aión* thus: *"The life of man, the time of life."* At this early date no theologian had yet imported into the word the meaning of endless duration. It retained only the sense it had in the classics, and in the Bible.

Theodoret[9] (A. D. 300-400) "*Aión* is not any existing thing, but an interval denoting time, sometimes infinite when spoken of God, sometimes proportioned to the duration of the creation, and sometimes to the life of man."

John of Damascus (A. D. 750,) says, "1, The life of every man is called *aión*. . . . 3, The whole duration or *life of this world* is called *aión*. 4, The life after the resurrection is called 'the *aión* to come.' "

But in the sixteenth century *Phavorinus* was compelled to notice an addition, which subsequently to the time of the famous Council of 544 had been grafted on the word. He says: "*Aión*, time, also life, also habit, or way of life. *Aión is also the eternal and endless*AS IT SEEMS TO THE THEOLOGIAN." Theologians had succeeded in using the word in the sense of endless, and Phavorinus was forced to recognize their usage of it and his phraseology shows conclusively enough that he attributed to theologians the authorship of that use of the word. Alluding to this definition, Rev. Ezra S. Goodwin, one of the ripest scholars and profoundest critics, says,(10) "Here I strongly suspect is the true secret brought to light of the origin of the sense of eternity in *aión*. *The theologian first thought he perceived it*, or else he placed it there. The theologian keeps it there, now. And the theologian will probably retain it there longer than any one else. Hence it is that those lexicographers who assign eternity as one of the meanings of *aión* uniformly appeal for proofs to either theological, Hebrew, or Rabbinical Greek, or some species of Greek subsequent to the age of the Seventy, if not subsequent to the age of the Apostles, so far a I can ascertain."

The second definition by *Phavorinus* is extracted literally from the "Etymologicon Magnum" of the ninth or tenth century. This gives us the usage from the fourth to the sixteenth century, and shows us that, if the word meant endless at the time of Christ, it must have changed from limited duration in the classics, to unlimited duration, and then back again, at the dates above specified!

From the sixteenth century onward, the word has been defined as used to denote all lengths of duration from brief to endless. We record here such definitions as we have found.

Rost: (German definitions) " *Aión*, duration, epoch, long time, eternity, memory of man, life-time, life, age of man. *Aiónios*, continual, always enduring, long continued, eternal."

Hedericus: "An age, eternity, an age a if always being; time of man's life in the memory of men, (wicked men, New Testament,) the spinal marrow. *Aiónios*, eternal, everlasting, continual."

Schleusner: "Any space of time whether longer or shorter, past, present or future, *to be determined by the persons or things spoken of, and the scope of the subjects;* the life or age of man. *Aiónios*, a definite and long period of time, that is, a *long enduring, but still definite period of time.*"

Passow: " *Aiónios,* long continued, eternal, everlasting, in the classics.

Grove: "Eternity; and age, life, duration, continuance of time; a revolution of ages, a dispensation of Providence, this world or life; the world or life to come. *Aiónios,* eternal, immortal, perpetual, former, past, *ancient.*"

Donnegan: "Time; space of time; life time and life; the ordinary period of man's life; the age of man; man's estate; a long period of time; eternity; the spinal marrow. *Aiónios,* of long duration, lasting, eternal, permanent."

Ewing: "Duration, finite or infinite; a period of duration, past or future; an age; duration of the world; ages of the world; human life in this world, or the next; our manner of life in the world; and age of divine dispensation, the ages, generally reckoned three, that before law, that under the law, and that under the Messiah. *Aiónios,* (from preceding,) ages of the world, periods of the dispensatins since the world began."

Schrevelius: "An age, a long period of time; *indefinite duration,* time, whether longer or shorter, past, prensent or future; also, in the New Testament, the wicked men of the age, life, the life of man. *Aiónios,* of long duration, lasting, sometimes everlasting, sometimes lasting through life as *æturnus* in Latin."

Dr. Taylor, who wrote the Hebrew Bible three times with his own hand, says of *Olam, (*Greek *Aión)* it signifies a duration which is concealed, as being of an unknown or great length. "It signifies eternity, *not from the proper force of the word, but when the sense of the place or the nature of the subject require it, as God and his attributes.*"

Pickering: Almost identical with Schrevelius in his definitions.

Hinks: "A period of time; and age, an after time, eternity.*Aiónios,* lasting, eternal, of old, since the beginning."

Lutz: "An age, time, eternity. *Aiónios,* durable, eternal."

Macknight: (Scotch Presbyterian.) "*These words being ambiguous, are always to be understood according to the nature and circumstances to which they are applied.*" He thinks the words sustain endless punishment, but adds: "At the same time I must be so candid as to acknowledge that the use of these terms, forever, eternal and everlasting, in other passages of Scripture, shows that *they who understand these words in a limited sense, when applied to punishment, put no forced interpretation upon them.*

Wright: "Time, age, life-time, period, revolution of ages, dispensation of Providence, present world, or life, world to come, eternity.*Aiónios*, eternal, ancient."

Robinson: "Life, also an age, that is an indefinite long period of time, perpetuity, ever, forever, eternity, forever, without end, to the remotest time, forever and ever, of old, from everlasting, the world, present or future, this world and the next, present world, men of this world, world itself, advent of Messiah. *Aiónios*, perpetual, everlasting, eternal, chiefly spoken of future time, ancient."

Jones: "An everlasting age, eternal, forever, a period of time, age, life, the present world, or life; the Jewish dispensation; a good demon, angel as supposed to exist forever . . . *Aiónios,* everlasting, ancient."

Schweighauser and *Valpyv* substantially agree.

Maclaine, in his Mosheim: *Aión* or *æon* among the ancients, was used to signify the *age of man, or the duration of human life.*"

Cruden: "The words eternal, everlasting, forever, are sometimes taken for a long time, and are not always to be understood strictly, for example, 'Thou shalt be our guide form this time forth, even forever,' that is, during our whole life."

Alex. Campbell: "ITS RADICAL IDEA IS INDEFINITE DURATION."

Whitby: "Nothing is more common and familiar in Scripture than to render a thorough and irreparable vastation, whose effects and signs should be still remaining, by the word *aiónios*, which we render eternal."*Hammond, Benson*, and *Gilpin*, in notes on Jude 7, say the same. Liddell and Scott also give to *aión*, in the poets the sense of life and lifetime, as also an age or generation.

Pearce (in Matt. vii:33) says: "The Greek word *aión*, seems to signify age here, as it often does in the New Testament, and according to *its most proper signification.*" *Clarke, Wakefield, Boothroyd, Simpson, Lindsey, Mardon, Acton*, agree. So do *Locke, Hammond, Le Clerc, Beausobre, Lenfant, Dodridge, Paulus, Kenrick and Olshausen.*

T. Southwood Smith: "Sometimes it signifies the term of human life; at other times an age, or dispensation of Providence. Its most common signification is that of age or dispensation."

Scarlett: "That *aiónion,* does not mean endless or eternal, may appear from considering that no adjective can have a greater force than the noun from which it is derived. If *aión* means age (which none either will or can deny) then *aiónionmust mean age-lasting,* or duration through the age or ages to which the thing spoken or relates."

Even Professor *Stuart* is obliged to say: "The most common and appropriate meaning of *aión* in the New Testament, and the one which corresponds with the Hebrew word *olam,* and which therefore deserves the first rank in regard to order, I put down first: *an indefinite period of time*; time without limitation; ever, forever, time without end, eternity, all in relation to future time. *The different shades by which the word is rendered, depend on the object with whichaiónios is associated,* or to which it has relation, rather than to any difference in the real meaning of the word."

J. W. Haley *says: "The Hebrew word 'olam' rendered 'forever,' does not imply the metaphysical idea of absolute endlessness, but a period of indefinite length, as Rambach says, a very long time, the end of which is hidden from us." Olam or olim is the Hebrew equivalent of *aión.*

Dr. Edward Beecher(11) remarks, "It commonly means merely continuity of action . . . all attempts to set forth eternity as the original and primary sense of *aión* are at war with the facts of the Greek language for five centuries, in which it denoted life and its derivative senses, and *the sense eternity was unknown.*" And he also says what is the undoubted fact, "that the original sense of*aión* is not eternity. . . . *It is conceded on all hands* that this (life) was originally the general use of the word. In the Paris edition of Henry Stephens' Lexicon it is affirmed emphatically "that life, or the space of life, is the primitive sense of the word, and that it is always so used by Homer, Hesiod, and the old poets; also by Pindar and the tragic writers, as well as by Herodotus and Xenophon." "Pertaining to the world to come," is the sense given to "These shall go away into everlasting punishment," by Prof. Tayler Lewis, who adds(12) "The preacher in contending with the Universalist and the Restorationist, would commit an error, and it may be suffer a failure in his argument, should he lay the whole stress of it on the etymological of historical significance of the words *aión*, *aiónios*, and attempt to prove that of themselves they necessarily carry the meaning of endless duration. 'These shall go away into the restraint, imprisonment of the world to come,' is all we can etymologically or exegetically make of the word in this passage."

* "An Examination of the Alleged Discrepancies of the Bible," p.216.

THE TRUE IDEA.

Undoubtedly the definition given by *Schleusner* is the accurate one, 'Duration determined by the subject to which it is applied.' Thus it only expresses the idea of endlessness when connected with what is endless, as God. The word great is an illustrative word. Great applied to a tree, or mountain, or man, denotes different degrees, all finite, but when referring to God, it has the sense of infinite. Infinity does not reside in the word great but it has that meaning when applied to God. It does not impart it to God, it derives it from him. So of *aiónion;* applied to Jonah's residence in the fish, it means seventy hours; to the priesthood of Aaron, it signifies several centuries; to the mountains, thousands of years; to the punishments of a merciful God, as long as is necessary to vindicate his law and reform his children; to God himself, eternity. What great is to size, *aiónios* is to duration. Human beings live from a few hours to a century; nations from a century to thousands of years; and worlds, for aught we know, from a few to many millions of years, and God is eternal. So that when we see the word applied to a human life it denotes somewhere from a few days to a hundred years; when it is applied to a nation, it denotes anywhere from a century to ten thousand years, more or less, and when to God it means endless. In other words it practically denotes indefinite duration, as we shall see when we meet the word in sacred and secular literature. Dr. Beecher well observes:

*"There are SIX AGES, or aggregates of ages, involving temporary systems, spoken of in the Old Testament. These ages are distinctly stated to be temporary, and yet to them all are applied *olam* and its reduplications, as fully and emphatically as they are to God. This is a positive demonstration that the word *olam*, as affirmed by Taylor and Fuerst in their Hebrew Concordances *means an indefinite period or*

*age, past or future, and not an absolute eternity. When applied to God, the*IDEA OF ETERNITY IS DERIVED FROM HIM, AND NOT FROM THE WORD. . . . This indefinite division of time is represented *olam* (Greek *aión*). Hence we find, since there are many ages, or periods, that the word is used in the plural. Moreover, since one great period or age can comprehend under it subordinate ages, we find such expressions as an age of ages, or an *olam* of *olams*, and other reduplications.

"In some cases, however, the reduplication of *olam* seems to be a rhetorical amplification of the idea, without any comprehension of ages by a greater age. This is especially true when *olam* is in the singular in both parts of the reduplication, as "To the age of the age."

"The use of the word in the plural is decisive evidence that the sense of the word is not eternity, in the absolute sense, for there can be but one such eternity. But as time past and future can be divided by ages, so there may be many ages, and an age of ages."

* Christian Union.

ETERNAL DURATION AND MODERN CONCEPTIONS.

It does not seem to have been generally considered by students of this subject that the thought of endless duration is comparatively a modern conception. The ancients, at a time more recent than the dates of the Old Testament, had not yet cognized the idea of endless duration, so that passages containing the word applied to God do not mean that he is of eternal duration, but the idea was of indefinite and not unlimited duration. I introduce here a passage from Professor Knapp, or Knappius, the author of the best edition of the Greek Testament known, and one in use in many colleges and ranks as a scholar of rare erudition. He observes:

"The pure idea of eternity is too abstract to have been conceived in the early ages of the world, and accordingly *is not found expressed by any word in the ancient languages*. But as cultivation advanced and this idea became more distinctly developed, it became necessary in order to express it to invent new words in a new sense, as was done with the words *eternitas,perennitas*, etc. The Hebrews were destitute of any single word to express endless duration. To express a past eternity they said before the world was; a future, when the world shall be no more. . . . *The Hebrews and other ancient people have no one word for expressing the precise idea of eternity.*"

AN IMPRESSIVE REFLECTION.

I pause here long enough to raise this question: Is it possible that our heavenly Father had created a world of endless torture, to which his children for thousands of years were crowding in myriads, and that he not only had not revealed the fact to them, but was so shortsighted that he had not given them a word to express the fact, or even a capacity sufficient to bring the idea of the eternal suffering to which they were liable, within the compass of the cognition? He created the horse for man's use, and created man capable of comprehending the horse; he surrounded him with multitudes of animate and inanimate objects, each of which he could name and comprehend, but the most important subject of all-one which must be believed in, or eternal woe is the penalty, he not only had no name for, but was incapable of the faintest conception of the mere fact! Would, or could a good Father be guilty of such an omission?

Can anything be clearer than this, that the lexicographers and critics unite in saying that limited duration is not only allowable, but that it is the prevailing signification of the word? Do they not agree that eternal duration is not in the word, and can only be imparted to it by the subject associated with it? Thus Lexicography declares that Limited Duration is the force of the word, duration to be determined by the subjected treated, if we allow Etymology and Lexicography to declare the verdict. And yet it is possible for these to be mistaken. Incredible, but still possible, that all students and critics of the word should have mistaken its character. But there is one tribunal that cannot mislead, and that is Usage.

III -- USAGE.

In tracing the usage of the word, our sources of information will be (1) The Greek Classics, (2) The Septuagint Old Testament, (3) Those Jewish Greeks nearly contemporary with Christ, (4) The New Testament, and (5) The Early Christian Church.

The Pentateuch was rendered into Greek at about the time of the return from the Babylonish Captivity, and the whole Old Testament, was combined into one collection about B.C. 200-300. At that time there was a large amount of Greek literature, now known as the Classics, and of course the Seventy gave to all Greek words their legitimate meaning, as found in the Classics. To ascertain just what the Greek Old Testament means by *Aión* or any other word, we need only learn its meaning in the Classics. They would as soon have rendered the Hebrew word for horse by a Greek word meaning fly, as they would have used*aión* for endless duration, if, as we shall show is the fact, antecedent Greek literature used it to denote limited duration.

1.-- THE GREEK CLASSICS.

It is a vital question *How was the word used in the Greek literature with which the Seventy were familiar, that is, the Greek Classics?*

Some years since Rev. Ezra S. Goodwin(13) patiently and candidly traced this word through the Classics, finding the noun frequently in nearly all the writers, but not meeting the adjective until Plato, its inventor, used it. He states, as the result of his protracted and exhaustive examination from the beginning down to Plato, "We have the whole evidence of seven Greek writers, extending through about six centuries, down to the age of Plato, who make use of *Aión*, in common with other words; and *no one of them*EVER employs *it in the sense of eternity.*"

When the Old Testament was translated from Hebrew into Greek by the Seventy, the word *aión* had been in common use for many centuries. It is preposterous to say that the Seventy would render the Hebrew *olam* by the Greek *aión* and give to the latter (1) a different meaning from that of the former, or (2) a different meaning from *aión* in the current Greek literature. It is self-evident, then, that *Aión* in the Old Testament means exactly what *Olam* means, and also what *Aión* means in the Greek classics. Indefinite duration is the sense of *olam*, and it is equally clear that *aión* has a similar signification.

In the Iliad and Odyssey *Aión* occurs thirteen times, as a noun, besides its occurrence as a participle in the sense of hearing, perceiving, understanding. *Homer never uses it as signifying eternal duration.* Priam to Hector says,(14) "Thyself shall be deprived of pleasant *aiónos*" (life.) Andromache over dead Hector,(15) "Husband thou hast perished from *aiónos*" (life or time.)

Dr. Beecher writes[16] "But there is a case that excludes all possibility of doubt or evasion, in the Homeric Hymn of Mercury, vs. 42 and 119. Here *aión* is used to denote the marrow as the *life* of an animal, as Moses calls the blood the life. This is recognized by Cousins in his Homeric Lexicon. In this case to pierce the life (*aión*) of a turtle means to pierce the spinal cord. The idea of *life* is here exclusive of time or eternity." These are fair illustrations of Homer's use of the word.

Hesiod employs it twice: "To him (the married man) during *aiónos* (life) evil is constantly striving, etc.[17] Æschulus has the word nineteen times, after this manner: "This life (*aión*) seems long, etc.[18] "Jupiter, king of the never-ceasing world."[19] *(aiónos apaustau.)*

Pindar gives thirteen instances, such as "A long life produces the four virtues."[20] *(Ela de kai tessaras aretas ho makros aión.)*

Sophocles nine times. "Endeavor to remain the same in mind as long as you live." *Askei toiaute noun di aiónos menein.*[21] He also employs *makraion* five times, as long-enduring. The word long increases the force of *aión*, which would be impossible if it had the idea of eternity.

Aristotle uses *aión* twelve times. He speaks of the existence or duration (*aión*) of the earth;[22] of an unlimited *aiónos*;[23] and elsewhere, he says: *aión sunekes kai aidios*, "an eternal *aión*" (or being) "pertaining to God." The fact that Aristotle found it necessary to add *aidios* to *aión* to ascribe eternity to God demonstrates that he found no sense of eternity in the word *aión*, and utterly discards the idea that he held the word to mean endless duration, even admitting that he derived it, or supposed the ancients did, from *aei ón* according to the opinion of some lexicographers.

A similar use of the word appears in de Cælo.[24] "The entire heaven is one and eternal (*aidios*) having neither beginning nor end of an entire *aión*." In the same work[25] occurs the famous passage where Aristotle has been said to describe the derivation of the word, which we have quoted on page 7, *Aión estin, apo tou aei einai.*

Mr. Goodwin well observes that the word had existed a thousand years before Aristotle's day, and that he had no knowledge of its origin, and poorer facilities for tracing it than many a scholar of the present, possesses. "While, therefore, we would regard an opinion of Aristotle on the derivation of an ancient word, with the respect due to extensive learning and venerable age, still we must bear in mind that his opinion is not indusputable authority." Mr. Goodwin proceeds to affirm that Aristotle does not apply *aei ón* to duration, but to God, and that (as we have shown) a human existence is an *Aión*. Completeness, whether brief or protracted, is his idea; and as Aristotle employed it "*Aión* did not contain the meaning of eternity."

Hippocrates. "A human *aión* is a seven days matter."

Empedocles, An earthly body deprived of happy life, (*aiónos*.)

Euripides uses the word thirty-two times. We quote three instances: (26) "Marriage to those mortals who are well situated is a happy *aión*."(27) "Every *aión* of mortals is unstable."(28) "Along *aión* has many things to say," etc.

Philoctetes. "He breathed out the *aióna*." Mr. Goodwin thus concludes his conscientious investigation of such of the Greek classics as he examined line by line, AION IN THESE WRITERS NEVER EXPRESSES POSITIVE ETERNITY."

In his Physic(29), Aristotle quotes a passage from Empedocles, saying that in certain cases "*aión* is not permanent."

AIONIOS.

Aiónios is found in none of the ancient classics above quoted. Finding it in Plato, Mr. Goodwin thinks that Plato coined it, and it had not come into general use, for even Socrates, the teacher of Plato, does not use it. *Aidios* is the classic word for endless duration.

Plato uses *aión* eight times, *aiónios* five, *diaiónios* once, and *makraión* twice. Of course if he regarded *aión* as meaning eternity he would not prefix the word meaning long, to add duration to it.

In all the above authors extending more than six hundred years, the word is never found. Of course it must mean the same as the noun that is its source. It having clearly appeared that the noun is uniformly used to denote limited duration, and never to signify eternity, it is equally apparent that the adjective must mean the same. The noun sweetness gives its flavor to its adjective, sweet. The adjective long means precisely the same as the noun length. When sweet stands for acidity, and long represents brevity, *aiónios* can properly mean eternal, derived from *aión*, which represents limited duration. To say that Plato, the inventor of the word, has used the adjective to mean eternal, when neither he nor any of his predecessors ever used the noun to denote eternity, would be to charge one of the wisest of men with etymological stupidity. Has he been guilty of such folly? How does he use the word?

PLATO'S USAGE.

1. He employs the noun as his predecessors did. I give an illustration*- "Leading a life (*aióna*) involved in troubles."

2. The Adjective.(30) Referring to certain souls in Hades, he describes them as in *aiónion* intoxication. But that he does not use the word in the sense of endless is evident from the Phædon, where he says, "It is a very ancient opinion that souls quitting this world, repair to the infernal regions, and *return after that, to live in this world.*" After the *aiónion* intoxication is over, they return to earth, which demonstrates that the world was not used by him as meaning endless. Again,(31) he speaks of that which is indestructible, (*anolethron*) and not *aiónion.* He places the two words in contrast, whereas, had he intended to use *aiónion* as meaning endless, he would have said indestructible *and aiónion.*

Once more,(32) Plato quotes four instances of *aión*, and three of *aiónios*, and one of*diaiónios* in a single passage, in contrast with *aidios* (eternal.) The gods he calls eternal, (*aidios*) but the soul and the corporeal nature, he says, are *aiónios*, belonging to time, and "all these," he says, "*are part of time.*" And he calls Time [*Kronos*] an *aiónios* image of *Aiónos*. Exactly what so obscure an author may mean here is not apparent, but one thing is perfectly clear, he cannot mean eternity and eternal by *aiónios* and *aiónion*, for nothing is wider from the fact than that fluctuating, changing Time, beginning and ending, and full of mutations, is an image of Eternity. It is in every possible particular its exact opposite.

In De Mundo,(33) Aristotle says: "Which of these things separately can be compared with the order of the heaven, and the relation of the stars, sun, and also the moon moving in most perfect measures *from one aión to another aión*,"- *ex aiónos eis eteron aióna*. Now even if Aristotle had said that the word was at first *derived* from two words that signify always being, his own *use* of it demonstrates that it had not that meaning then [B.C. 350.] Again,(34) he says of the earth, "All these things seem to be done for her good, in order to maintain safety during her *aiónos*," duration, or life. And still more to the purpose is this quotation concerning God's existence.[(35)] Life and *an aión*CONTINUOUS AND ETERNAL, "*zoe kai aión, sunekes kai aidios, etc.*" Here the word *aidios*, [eternal] is employed to qualify *aión* and impart to it what it had not of itself, the sense of eternal. Aristotle could be guilty of no such language as "an eternal eternity." Had the word *aión* contained the idea of eternity in his time, or in his mind, he would not have added *aidios*. "For the limit enclosing the *time of the life* of every man, . . . is called his continuous existence, *aión*. On the same principle, the limit of the whole heaven, and the limit enclosing the universal system, is the divine and immortal ever-existing *aión*, deriving the name *aión* from ever-existing [*aei ón.*]"[(36)] In eleven out of twelve instances in the works of Aristotle, *aión* isused either doubtfully, or in a manner similar to the instance abovc cited, [from one *aión* to another, that is, from one age to another,] but in this last instance it is perfectly clear that an *aión* is only without end when it is described by and adjective like *aidios*, whose meaning is endless. Nobody cares how the word originated, after hearing from Aristotle himself that created objects exist from one *aión* to another, and that the existence of the eternal God is not described by a word so feeble, but by the addition of another that expresses endless duration. Here *aión* only obtains the force of eternal duration by being reinforced by the word immortal. If it meant eternity, the addition of immortal is like adding gilding to refined gold, and daubing paint on the petal of the lily.

In most of these the word is enlarged by descriptive adjectives. Æschylus calls Jupiter "king of *the never-ceasing aión*," and Aristotle expressly states in one case that the *aión* of heaven "has neither beginning nor end," and in another instance he calls man's life his *aión*, and the *aión* of heaven "immortal." If *aión* denotes eternity, why add "neither beginning nor end," or "immortal," to describe its meaning? These quotations unanswerable show that *aión* in the Classics, never means eternity unless a qualifying word or subject connected with it add to its intrinsic value.

Says Dr. Beecher: In Rome there were certain periodical games known as the *secular* games, from the Latin *seculum*, a period, or age.

The historian, Herodian, writing in Greek, calls these *aiónian* games, that is, periodical, occurring at the end of a seculum. It would be singular, indeed, to call them eternal or everlasting games. Cremer, in his masterly Lexicon of New Testament Greek, states the general meaning of the word to be 'Belonging to the *aión*.'" Herodotus, Isocrates, Xenophon, Sophocles, Diodorus Siculus use the word in precisely the same way. Diodorus Siculus says *ton apéiron aióna*, "indefinite time."

* De Legib. Lib. iii.

THE CLASSICS NEVER USE AION TO DENOTE ETERNITY.

It appears, then, that the classic Greek writers, for more than six centuries before the Septuagint was written, used the word *aión* and its adjective, but never once in the sense of endless duration.

When, therefore, the Seventy translated the Hebrew Scriptures into Greek, what meaning must they have intended to give to these words? It is not possible, it is absolutely insupposable that they used them with any other meaning than that which they had held in the antecedent Greek literature. As the Hebrew word meaning horse, was rendered by a Greek word meaning horse, as each Hebrew word was exchanged for a Greek word denoting precisely the same thing, so the terms expressive of duration in Hebrew became Greek terms expressing a similar duration. The translators consistently render *olam* by *aión*, both denoting indefinite duration.

We have shown, p. 18, that the idea of eternity had not entered the Hebrew mind when the Old Testament was written. How then could it employ terms expressive of endless duration? We have now shown that the Greek literature uniformly understands the word in the sense of limited duration. This teaches us exactly how the word was taken at the time the Septuagint was prepared, and shows us how to read understandingly the Old Testament.

When at length the idea of eternity was cognized by the human mind, probably first by the Greeks, what word did they employ to represent the idea? Did they regard *aión-aiónion* as adequate? Not at all, but Plato and Aristotle and others employ *aidios*, and distinctly use it in contrast with our mooted word. We have instanced Aristotle, (37) "The entire heaven is one and eternal [*aidios*] having neither beginning nor end of a complete *aión*, [life, or duration.]" In the same chapter*aidiotes* is used to mean eternity.

Plato,(38) calls the gods *aidion*, and their essence *aidion*, in contrast with temporal matters, which are *aiónios*. *Aidios* then, is the favorite word descriptive of endless duration in the Greek writers contemporary with the Septuagint.*Aión* is never thus used.

When, therefore, the Seventy translated the Hebrew Scriptures into Greek they must have used this word with the meaning it had whenever they had found it in the Greek classics. To accuse them of using it otherwise is to charge them with an intention to mislead and deceive.

Mr. Goodwin well observes: "Those lexicographers who assign eternity as one of the meanings of *aión*, uniformly appeal for proofs to either theological, Hebrew or Rabbinnical Greek, or some species of Greek subsequent to the age of the Seventy, if not subsequent to the age of the apostles, so far as I can ascertain. I do not know of an instance in which any lexicographer has produced the usage of *ancient* classical Greek, in evidence that *aión* means eternity. ANCIENT CLASSICAL GREEK REJECTS IT ALTOGETHER. . . . " By ancient he means the Greek existing in ages anterior to the days of the Seventy.

Thus it appears that when the Seventy began their work of giving the world a Greek version of the Old Testament that should convey the exact sense of the Hebrew Bible, they must have used *aión* in the sense in which it then was used. Endless duration is not the meaning the word had in Greek literature at that time. Therefore the word cannot have that meaning in the Old Testament Greek. Nothing can be plainer than that Greek Literature at the time the Hebrew Old Testament was rendered into the Greek Septuagint did not give to *Aión* the meaning of endless duration. Let us then consider the Old Testament Usage.

2.-- THE OLD TESTAMENT USAGE.

We have concluded, *a priori*, that the Old Testament must employ the word *Aión* in the sense of indefinite duration, because that was the uniform meaning of the word in all antecedent and contemporaneous Greek literature. Otherwise the Old Testament would mislead its readers. We now proceed to show that such is the actual usage of the word in the Old Testament.

And let us pause a moment on the brink of our investigation to speak of the utter absurdity of the idea that God has hung the great topic of the immortal welfare of millions of souls on the meaning of a single equivocal word. Had he intended to teach endless punishment by one word, that word would have been so explicit and uniform and frequent that no mortal could mistake its meaning. It would have stood unique and peculiar among words. It would no more be found conveying a limited meaning than is the sacred name of Jehovah applied to any finite being. Instead of denoting every degree of duration, as it does, it never would have meant less than eternity. The thought that God has suspended the question of man's final destiny on such a word would seem too preposterous to be entertained by any reflecting mind, did we not know that such an idea is held by Christians.

Endless duration is never expressed or implied in the Old Testament by *Aión* or any of its derivatives, except in instances where it acquires that meaning from the subject connected with it.

How is it used? Let us adduce a few illustrative

EXAMPLES.

Gen. vi:4, "There were giants in the earth in those days; and also after that, when the sons of God came in unto the daughters of men, and they bare children to them, the same became mighty men which were of old, (*aiónos*), men of renown." Gen. ix:12; God's covenant with Noah was "for *perpetual* (*aiónious*) generations." Gen. ix:16; The rainbow is the token of "the everlasting (*aiónion*) covenant" between God and "all flesh that is upon the earth." Gen. xiii:15; God gave the land to Abram and his seed "forever," (*aiónos*). Dr. T. Clowes says of this passage that it signifies the duration of human life, and he adds, "Let no one be surprised that we use the word *Olam* (*Aión*) in this limited sense. This is one of the most usual significations of the Hebrew *Olam* and the Greek *Aión*." In Isa. lviii:12; it is rendered "*old*" and "*foundations*," (*aiónioi* and *aiónia*). "And they that shall be of thee shall build the *old* waste places; thou shalt raise up the *foundations* of many generations; and thou shalt be called, The repairer of the breach." In Jer. xviii:15, 16, *ancient* and *perpetual*, (*aiónious* and *aiónion*). "Because my people hath forgotten me, they have burned incense to vanity, and they have caused them to stumble in their ways from the ancient paths, to walk in paths, in a way not cast up; to make their land desolate, and a perpetual hissing; every one that passeth thereby shall be astonished, and wag his head." Such instances may be cited to an indefinite extent. Ex. xv:18, "forever and ever and further," (*ton aióna, kai ep aióna, kai eti.*) Ex. xii:17, "And ye shall observe the feast of unleavened bread; for in this selfsame day have I brought your armies out of the land of Egypt, therefore shall ye observe this day in your generations by an ordinance forever," (*aiónion*). Numb. x:8, "And the sons of Aaron the priests, shall blow with the trumpets; and they shall be to you for an ordinance *forever* (*aiónion*) THROUGHOUT YOUR GENERATIONS." "Your generations," is here idiomatically given as the precise equivalent of "forever." Canaan was given as an "*everlasting* (*aiónion*) possession;" (Gen. xvii:8, xlviii:4; Lev. xxiv:8,9;) the hills are everlasting (*aiónioi*;) (Hab. iii:6;) the priesthood of Aaron (Ex. xl:15; Numb. xxv:13; Lev. xvi:34;) was to exist *forever*, and continue through *everlasting* duration; Solomon's temple was to last *forever*, (1 Chron. xvii:12;) though it was long since ceased to be; slaves were to remain in bondage *forever*, (Lev. xxv:46;) though every fiftieth year all Hebrew servants were to be set at liberty, (Lev. xxv: 10;) Jonah suffered an imprisonment behind the everlasting bars of earth, (Jon. ii:6;) the smoke of Idumea was to ascend *forever*, (Isa. xxxiv:10;) though it no longer rises, to the Jews God says (Jer. xxxii: 40;) "and I will bring an *everlasting* reproach upon you, and a *perpetual* shame, which shall not be forgotten," and yet, after the fullness of the Gentiles shall come in, Israel will be restored. Rom. xi: 25-6.

Not only in all these and multitudes of other cases does the word mean limited duration, but it is also used in the plural, thus debarring it from the sense of endless, as there can be but one eternity. In Dan. xii:3; the literal reading, if we allow the word to mean eternity, is "to *eternities and farther*," (*eis tous aiónas kai eti.*) Micah iv:5, "We will walk in the name of the Lord our God to eternity, and beyond," *eis ton aióna kai epekeina*. Ps. cxix:43-4, "And take not the word of truth utterly out of my mouth; for I have hoped in thy judgments. So shall

I keep thy law continually *forever and ever*." This is the strongest combination of the aionian phraseology: *eis ton aióna kai eis ton aióna tou aiónos,* and yet it is David's promise of fidelity as long as he lives among them that "reproach" him, in "the house of his pilgrimage." Ps. cxlviii:4-6, "Praise him, ye heaven of heavens, and ye waters that be above the heavens. Let them praise the name of the LORD: for he commanded and they were created. He hath also established them for *ever and ever:* he hath made a decree which shall not pass. The sun and moon, the stars of light, and even the waters above the heavens are established *forever*," *eis ton aióna tou aiónos*, and yet the firmament is one day to become as a folded garment, and the orbs of heaven are to be no more. Endless duration is out of the question in these and many similar instances.

In Lam. v:19, "forever and ever" is used as the equivalent of "from generation to generation." Joel ii:26-27, "And ye shall eat in plenty, and be satisfied, and praise the name of the LORD your God, that hath dealt wondrously with you: and my people shall *never* be ashamed. And ye shall know that I am in the midst of Israel, and that I am the Lord your God and none else: and my people shall *never* be ashamed." This is spoken of the Jewish nation. Isa. lx:15, "Whereas thou hast been forsaken and hated, so that no man went through thee, I will make thee an *eternal* (*aiónion*) excellency, a joy of many generations." Here many generations and eternal are exact equivalents. 1 Sam. i:22, "But Hannah went not up: for she said unto her husband, I will not go up until the child be weaned, and then I will bring him, that he may appear before the LORD, and there abide *forever*." The remaining of Samuel in the temple was to be "forever" (*aiónos*) 2 Kings, v:27, "The leprosy therefore of Naaman shall cleave unto thee, and unto thy seed *forever*." (*ton aióna*). Undoubtedly the seed of Gehazi is still on earth: but whether so or not the leprosy has departed. Daniel ii:4, "Then spake the Chaldeans to the king in Syriac, O king, live forever: *eis tous aióna*." The Chaldean's live forever meant precisely what the French *Vive*, and the English "Long live the King" mean. Eternal duration never entered the thought. Jerem. xvii:25, "Then shall there enter into the gates of this city kings and princes sitting upon the throne of David, riding in chariots and on horses, they, and their city shall remain *forever*," *eis ton aióna*. Eternity was not promised here. Long duration is the extent of the promise. Josh. iv:7, "Then ye shall answer them, That the waters of Jordan were cut off before the ark of the covenant of the LORD: when it passed over Jordan, the waters of Jordan were cut off; and these stones shall be for a memorial unto the children of Israel *forever*," *tou aiónos*. These stones are no longer a memorial. *This* forever has ended.

Forever and ever is applied to the hosts of heaven, or the sun, moon, and stars: to a writing contained in a book; to the smoke that went up from the burning land of Idumea; and to the time the Jews were to dwell in Judea.(39) The word *never* is applied to the time the sword was to remain in the house of David, to the time the Jews should experience shame.(40)

"*Everlasting*"(41) is applied to God's covenant with the Jews; to the priesthood of Aaron; to the statutes of Moses; to the time the Jews were to possess the land of Canaan; to the mountains and hills; and to the doors of the Jewish temple.(42) The word *forever* is applied to the duration of man's earthly existence; to the time a child was to abide in the temple; to the continuance of Gehazi's leprosy; to the duration of the life of David; to the duration of a king's life; to the duration of the earth; to the time the Jews were to possess the land of Canaan; to the time they were to dwell in Jerusalem; to the time a servant was to abide with his master; to the time Jerusalem was to remain a city; to the duration of the Jewish temple; to the laws and ordinances of Moses; to the time David was to be king over Israel; to the throne of Solomon; to the stones that were set up at Jordan; to the time the righteous were to inhabit the earth; and to the time Jonah was in the fish's belly.(43)

And yet, the land of Cannan, the Jews' "everlasting possession," has passed from their hand; the convenant of circumcision, an "everlasting covenant" was abolished almost two thousand years ago; the Jewish atonement (Lev. xvi,) an everlasting statute, is abrogated by the atonement of Christ; David was never to want a man to sit on Israel's throne. This aionian line of succession was long ago broken.

We have found the noun *Aión* three hundred and ninety-four times in the Old Testament, and the adjective *Aiónion* one hundred and ten times, and in all but four times it is the translation of *Olam*.

THE NOUN.

Waiving the passages where it is applied to God, and where by accommodation it may be *allowed* to imply endlessness, just as great applied to God means infinity, let us consult the general usage: Eccl. i:10, "Is there anything whereof it may be said, See, this is new! It hath been already of *old time*, which was before us." Ps. xxv:6, "Remember, O LORD, thy tender mercies and thy loving kindnesses; for they have been *ever of old*," (*aiónos*). Ps. cxix:52, "I remembered thy judgements*of old*, O LORD; and have comforted myself." Isa. xlvi:9, "Remember the former things *ofold*." Isa. lxiv:4, "Since the *beginning of the world*," (*aiónos*). Jer. xxviii:8, "The prophets that have been before me and before thee *of old* prophesied both against many countries, and against great kingdoms, of war, and of evil, and of pestilence." Jer. ii:20, "For *of old time* I have broken thy yoke, and burst thy bands." Prov. viii:23, "I (wisdom) was set up from everlasting (*aiónos*) from the beginning, or ever the earth was." Here *aiónos* and "before the world was, " are in apposition. Ps. lxxiii:12, "Behold, these are the ungodly, who prosper in the world," (time, *aiónos*.) Deut. xxxii:7, "Remember the days of *old*." Ezek. xxvi:20, "The people of *old time*." Ps. cxliii:3, "Those who have been *long* dead." --Same in Lam. iii:6. Amos ix:11, "Days *ofold*." Isa. i:9, "Generations*ofold*." Micah vii:14, "Days *ofold*." Same in Malachi iii:4. Ps. xlviii:14, "For this God is our God *for ever and ever*: he will be our guide even unto death." This plural form denotes "even unto death." Christ's kingdom is prophesied as destined to endure "forever," "without end," etc. Dan. ii:44; Isa. lix:21; Ps. cx:4; Isa. ix:7; Ps. lxxxix:29. Now if anything is taught in the Bible, it is that Christ's kingdom shall end. In 1 Corin. xv: it is expressly and explicitly declared that Jesus shall surrender the kingdom to God the Father, that his reign shall entirely cease. Hence, when we read in such passages as Dan. ii:44, that Christ's kingdom shall stand forever, we must understand that the forever denotes the reign of Messias, bounded by "the end," when God shall be "all in all."

Servants were declared to be bound forever, when all servants were emancipated every fifty years. Thus in Deut. xv:16,17, we read, "And it shall be, if he say unto thee, I will not go away from thee; because he loveth thee and thine house, because he is well with thee, then thou shalt take an awl, and thrust it through his ear unto the door, and he shall be thy servant forever." And yet we are told, Lev. xlv: 10,39,41, "And ye shall hallow the fiftieth year, and proclaim liberty throughout all the land unto all the inhabitants thereof: it shall be a jubilee unto you; and ye shall return every man unto his possession, and ye shall return every man unto his family. And if thy brother that dwelleth with thee be waxen poor, and be sold unto thee; thou shalt not compel him to serve as a bond servant, but as a hired servant, and as a sojourner, he shall be with thee, and shall serve thee unto the year of jubilee: and then shall he depart from thee, both he and his children with him, and shall return unto his own family, and unto the possession of his father shall he return." This forever at the utmost could only be forty-nine years and three hundred and sixty-four days and some odd hours. And certainly no one will ascribe endless duration to *aión* in the following passages: II Sam. vii:16,29; I Ki. ii: 45, and ix:5; I Chron. xvii:27, and xxviii:4; II Chron. xiii:5; Psa. lxxxix:4,336,37; Ezek. xxxvii:25; I Sam. xiii:13; II Sam. vii: 13,16,25,26; xxii:51; I Ki. ii:33; I Chron. xvii:12,14,14,23, and xxii: 10, xxviii:7; Psa. xviii:50, lxxxix:4, and cxxxii:12; Ex. xxxii:13, Josh. xiv:9; I Chron. xx:7; Jud. ii:1; II Ch. vii:3; Psa. cv:8; Gen. xiii:15; I Ch. xxviii:4,7,8; Jer. xxxi:40; Ezek. xxxvii:25; Jer. vii:7,7; II Sa. vii:24; I Chron. xvii:22; Joel iii:20; II Ki. xxi:7; II Chron. xxxiii:4; Psa. xlviii: 8; Jer. xvii:25; I Chron. xxiii:25; Isa. xxviii:7; I Ki. ix:3; II Chron. xxx: 8; Ezek. xxxvii:26,28; II Chron. vii:16; Ex. xix:9, and xl:15; I Chron. xxiii:23, 13; I Chron. xv:2; Lev. iii:17; II Chron. ii:4; Ex. xii:24; Josh. iv:7; Am. i:11; Isa. xiii:20; Isa. xxxiii:20, xxxiv:10; I Ki. x:9; II Chron. ix:8; Psa. cii:28; Ezek. xliii:7.

Many passages allude to the earth as enduring forever -- to the grave, as man's "long home," to God's existence, as "Forever, etc." Often the language is equivalent to "to the ages," or "from age to age," and sometimes eternal duration is predicated, *never* because the word compels it, but because the theme treated requires it.

THE ADJECTIVE

is applied to God, Zion, and things intrinsically endless, and thus acquires from the connected subjects a meaning not inherent in the word, as in the following passages: Gen. xxi:33; Ex. iii:15; Job xxxiii:

12; Isa. xl:28, li:11, liv:8, lv:3,13, lvi:5; lx:15,19, lxi:7,8; lxiii:12; Ezek. xxxvii:26; Dan. vii:27, ix:24, xii:2; Hab. iii:6; Ps. cxii:6, cxxx:8.

THE ADJECTIVE LIMITED.

But it is found with limited meaning in these and other passages: Gen. ix:12-16; Gen. xvii:8,13,19; and Num. xxv:13; Ex. xii:14,17; xxvii:21; xxviii:43; xxix:28; xxx:21; xxxi:16,17; Lev. vi:18,22; vii: 34,36; x:15; xvi:29,31,34; xvii:7; xxiii:14,31,41; xxiv:3,8,9. Num. x: 8; xv:15; xviii:8,11,19,23; xix:10,21; II Sam. xxiii:5; I Chron. xvi:17; Isa. xxiv:5; Ezek. xvi:60; Psa. lxxvii:5; Isa lxiii:11; Jer. vi:16; xviii:15; Job xxi:11; xxii:15; Isa. lviii:12; lxi:4; Ezek. xxvi:20; Prov. xxii:28; xxiii:10; Ezek. xxxvi:2; xxxv:5; Isa. liv:4; Jer. v:22; xviii:16; xxv:9,12; Ezek. xxxv:9; Jer. xx:17; xxiii:40; li:39; Micah ii:9.

Let us quote some of the foregoing texts: "And ye shall observe the feast of unleavened bread; for in this selfsame day have I brought your armies out of the land of Egypt: therefore shall ye observe this day in your generations by an ordinance for ever." "And thou shalt command the children of Israel, that they bring thee pure olive beaten for the light, to cause the lamp to burn always." "In the tabernacle of the congregation without the veil, which is before the testimony, Aaron and his sons shall order it from evening to morning before the Lord: *it shall be* a statute *for ever*UNTO THEIR GENERATIONS on behalf of the children of Israel." "And they shall be upon Aaron and upon his sons, when they come in unto the tabernacle of the congregation, or when they come near unto the altar to minister in the holy place; that they bear not iniquity and die: it shall be a statute *for ever* unto him and his seed after him." "Hast thou not marked the *old* way which wicked men have trodden?" "Fear ye not me: saith the Lord: will ye not tremble at my presence, which have placed the sand for the bound of the sea by a *perpetual* decree, that it cannot pass it: and though the waves thereof toss themselves, yet can they not prevail; though they roar, yet can they not pass over it?"

To render the word eternal will show how absurd that definition is, in the following passages[(44)]:

"I will give unto thee, and thy seed after thee, the land wherin thou art a stranger, all the land of Canaan, for an *eternal* possession." "And thou shalt anoint them as thou didst their father, that they surely be a

priesthood through the *eternity*." "Then his master shall bring him to the door, or unto the door-posts, and his master shall bore his ear through with an awl, and he shall serve him through the *eternity*."
"The water compassed me about --even to the soul;
The weeds were wrapped about my head,
I went down to the bottoms of the bountains;
The earth with her *eternal* bars was about me."

Still further do the subjoined texts demonstrate the impropriety of the popular rendering, which would compel us to read[45]: "The Lord shall reign *to* the *eternity*, and *during* the *eternity*, and LONGER." "And they that be wise shall shine as the brightness of the firmament; and they that turn many to righteousness as the stars through the *eternities* and *longer*." "And we will walk in the name of Jehovah our God through the *eternity* and *longer*." But substitute ages and the sense is perfect. Ex. xv:18, "The Lord shall reign from age to age, and *beyond all the ages*;" Dan. xii:3, "*Through the ages and beyond them all*;" Micah iv:5, "*Through the age and beyondit*."

No one can read the Old Testament carefully and unbiassed, and fail to see that the word has a great range of meaning, bearing some such relation to duration as the word great does to size. We say God is infinite when we call him the Great God, not because great means infinite, but because God is infinite. The *aiónion* God is of eternal duration, but the *aiónion* smoke of Idumea has expired, and the *aiónion* hills will one day crumble, and all merely aionian things will cease to be.

While it is a rule of language that adjectives qualify and describe nouns, it is no less true that nouns modify adjectives. A tall flower, a tall dog, a tall man, and a tall tree are of different degrees of length, though the different nouns are described by the same adjective. The adjective is in each instance modified by its noun, just as the aionian bars that held Jonah three days, and the aionian priesthood of Aaron already ended, and the aionian hills yet to be destroyed, and aionian punishment, always proportioned to human guilt, are of different degrees of length. The adjective is modified and its length is determined by the noun with which it is connected.

THE SUBJECT DETERMINES THE DURATION DESCRIBED BY THE ADJECTIVE.

Prof. Tayler Lewis says, "'One generation passeth away, and another generation cometh; but the earth abideth forever.' This certainly indicates, not an endless eternity in the strictest sense of the word, but only a future of unlimited length. Ex. xxxi:16; 'Wherefore the children of Israel shall keep the Sabbath, to observe the Sabbath throughout their generations, for a *perpetual* covenant.' *Olam* here would seem to be taken as a hyperbolical term for indefinite or unmeasured duration." Where the context demands it, as "I live forever," spoken of God, he says it means endless duration, for "*it is the subject to which it is applied that forces to this, and*NOT*any etymological necessity in the word itself.*" He adds that *Olam* and *Aion*, in the plural, ages, and ages of ages, demonstrate that neither of the words, of itself, denotes eternity. He admits that they are used to give an idea of eternity, but that applied to God and his kingdom, the ages are finite[(46)]. Prof. L. is eminently learned and as eminently orthodox.

THE END OF AIONIAN THINGS.

Now the Jews have lost their eternal excellency; Aaron and his sons have ceased from their priesthood; the Mosaic system is superseded by Christianity; the Jews no longer possess Canaan; David and his house have lost the throne of Israel; the Jewish temple is destroyed, and Jerusalem is wiped out as the holy city; the servants who were to be bondmen forever are all free from their masters; Gehazi is cured of his leprosy; the stones are removed from Jordan, and the smoke of Idumea no longer rises; the righteous do not posses the land promised them forever; some of the hills and mountains have fallen, and the tooth of Time will one day gnaw the last of them into dust; the fire has expired from the Jewish altar; Jonah has escaped from his imprisonment; all these and numerous other eternal, everlasting things -- things that were to last forever, and to which the various aionian words are applied -- have now ended, and if these hundreds of instances must denote limited duration why should the few times in which punishments are spoken of have any other meaning? Even if endless duration were the intrinsic meaning of the word, all intelligent readers of the Bible would perceive that the word must be employed to denote limited duration in the passages above cited. And surely in the very few times in which it is connected with punishment it must have a similar meaning. For who administers this punishment? Not a monster, not an infinite devil, but a God of love and mercy, and the same common sense that would forbid us to give the word the meaning of endless duration, were that its literal meaning, when we see it applied to what we know has ended, would forbid us to give it that meaning when applied to the dealings of an Infinite Father with an erring and beloved child. But when we interpret it in the light of its lexicography, and general usage out of the Old Testament, and perceive that it only has the sense of endless when the subject compels it [emphasized by editor], as when referring to God, we see that it is a species of blasphemy to allow that it denotes endless duration when describing God's punishments.

APPLIED TO PUNISHMENT.

A few prominent instances illustrate the usage of the word connected with punishment. Ps. ix:5, "Thou *hast* destroyed the wicked." How? The explanation follows: "Thou hast *put out their name forever and ever*," (*ton aiona, kai eis ton aióna tou aionos.*) His is not endless torment, but oblivion. Solomon elsewhere observes: Prov. x:7, "The name of the wicked shall rot," while David says, Ps. cxii:6, "The righteous shall be in everlasting remembrance." Ps. lxxviii:66, "He put them (his enemies) to a perpetual reproach." Is. xxxiii:14, "Who among us shall dwell with the devouring fire? Who among us shall dwell with everlasting burnings?" The prophet is here speaking of God's temporal judgments, represented by fire. "The earth mourneth; Lebanon is ashamed; the people shall be as the burnings of lime." Who will dwell in safety amid these fiery judgments? These aionian burnings? "He that walks uprightly." Earthly judgements among which the upright are to dwell in safety are here described, and not endless fire hereafter. Jer. xvii:4, "Ye have kindled a fire in mine anger which shall burn forever." Where was this to be? The preceding verse informs us. "I will cause thee to serve thine enemies in a land which thou knowest not." Jer. xxiii:40, "I will bring an everlasting reproach upon you; and a perpetual shame which shall not be forgotten." The connection fully explains this verse 39, "I will utterly forget you, and I will forsake you, and the city that I gave you and your fathers. See Jer. xx:11. Mal. i:4, "The people against whom the Lord hath indignation forever." This is an announcement of God's judgements on Edom" "They shall build but I will throw down" and they shall call them the border of wickedness, and the people against whom the Lord hath indignation forever."

EVERLASTING SHAME AND CONTEMPT.

Dan. xii:2, "And many of them that sleep in the dust of the earth shall awake, some to everlasting life, and some to shame and everlasting contempt." When was this to take place? "At that time." What time? Verse 31, chap. xi, speaks of the coming of the "abomination that maketh desolate." Jesus says, Matt. xxiv:15,16, Luke xxi:20,21, "When ye therefore (the disciples) shall see the abomination of desolation, spoken of by Daniel the prophet stand in the holy place, then let them which be in Judea flee to the mountains. And when ye shall see Jerusalem compassed with armies, then know that the desolation thereof is nigh. Then let them which are in Judea flee to the mountains; and let them which are in the midst of it depart out; and let not them that are in the countries enter thereinto." Daniel says this was to be (xii:7) "When he shall have accomplished to scatter the power of the holy people." Jesus says, "For then shall be great tribulations, such as was not since the beginning of the world to this time; no, nor ever shall be." And when that was Jesus tells us: "this generation shall not pass away, till all these things be fulfilled." The events discussed in Daniel are the same as those in Matt. xxiv, and came in this world in the generation that crucified Jesus.

DUST OF THE EARTH. The phrase sleeping in the dust of the earth, is of course employed figuratively, to indicate sloth, spiritual lethargy, as in Ps. xliv:25; Isa. xxv:12; xxvi:5; I Tim. v:6; Rev. iii:1, "For our soul is bowed down to the dust." "And the fortress of the high fort of thy walls shall he bring down, lay low, and bring to the ground, even to the dust." "For he bringeth down them that dwell on high; the lofty city, he layeth it low; he layeth it low, even to the ground; he bringeth it even to the dust." "But she that liveth in pleasure is dead while she liveth." "I know thy works; that thou hast a name, and that thou livest and art dead."

It was a prophecy of the moral awakening that came at the time of the advent of Jesus, and was then fulfilled. When we come to Matt. xxiv and xxv we shall see the exact nature of this judgment. Walter Balfour describes it,[(47)] "They," (those who obeyed the call of Jesus) "heard the voice of the Son of God, and lived." See John v: 21,25,28,29, Eph. v:14. The rest kept on till the wrath of God came on them to the uttermost. They all, at last, awoke; but it was to shame and everlasting contempt, in being dispersed among all nations, and they have become a by-word and an hissing even unto this day. Jeremiah in chapter xxiii:39,40, predicted this very punishment and calls it an "everlasting reproach and a perpetual shame."

These few passages, not one of which conveys a hint of endless punishment, are all that connect our word denoting duration with punishment in the Old Testament.

Out of more than five hundred occurrences of our disputed word in the Old Testament, more than four hundred denote limited duration, so that the great preponderance of Old Testament usage fully agrees with the Greek classics. The remaining instances follow the rule given by the best lexicographers, that it only means endless when it derives its meaning or endlessness from the nature of the subject with which it is connected.

Dr. Beecher(48) remarks that the sense of endless given to the aionian phraseology "fills the Old Testament with contradictions, for it would make it declare the absolute eternity of systems which it often and emphatically declares to be temporary. Nor can it be said that *aiónios* denotes lasting as long as the nature of things permits. The Mosaic ordinances might have lasted at least to the end of the world, but did not. Moreover, on this principle the exceptions to the true sense of the word exceed its proper use; for *in the majority of cases in the Old Testament aiónios is applied to that which is limited and temporary.*"

Now if endless punishment awaits millions of the human race, and if it is denoted by this word, is it possible that only David, Isaiah, Jeremiah, Daniel, and Malachi use the word to define punishment, in all less than a dozen times, while Job, Moses, Joshua, Ruth, Ezra, Nehemiah, Esther, Solomon, Ezekiel, Hosea, Joel, Amos, Obadiah, Jonah, Micah, Nahum, Habbakkuk, Zephaniah, Haggai, and Zachariah never employ it thus? Such silence is criminal, on the popular hypothesis. These holy men should and would have made every sentence bristle with the word, and thus have borne the awful message to the soul with an emphasis that could be neither resisted nor disputed. The fact that the word is so seldom, and by so few applied to punishment, and never in the Old Testament to punishment beyond death, demonstrates that it cannot mean endless.

TESTIMONY OF SCHOLARS.

The best critics concede that the doctrine of endless punishment is not taught in the Old Testament. But the word in dispute is found in connection with punishment in the Old Testament. This is a concession that the word has no such meaning in the Old Testament. Milman: "The lawgiver (Moses) maintains a profound silence on that fundamental article, if not of political, at least of religious legislation -- rewards and punishments in another life." Paley, Jahn, Whately are to the same purport, and H. W. Beecher says, "If we had only the Old Testament we could not tell if there were any future punishment."(49)

We should then conclude that the word means one thing in the Old Testament and another in the New, did we not find that the same meaning continues in the New that we have found to prevail uniformly in the Old Testament, and in antecedent and contemporaneous Greek literature.

THREE QUESTIONS

Here press the mind with irresistible force, and they can only receive one answer. 1st, Had God intended endless punishment, would the Old Testament have failed to reveal it? 2d, If God does not announce it in the Old Testament, is it supposable that he has revealed it elsewhere: 3d, Would he for thousands of years conceal so awful a destiny from millions whom he had created and exposed to it? No child of God ought to be willing to impeach his Heavenly Father by withholding an indignant negative to these questions.

3. -- JEWISH GREEK USAGE.

Those Jews who were contemporary with Christ, but who wrote in Greek, will teach us how they understood the word. Of course when Jesus used it, he employed it as they understood it.

Josephus(50) applies the word to the imprisonment to which John the tyrant was condemned by the Romans; to the reputation of Herod; to the everlasting memorial erected in re-building the temple, already destroyed, when he wrote; to the everlasting worship in the temple which, in the same sentence he says was destroyed; and he styles the time between the promulgation of the law and his writing a long*aión*. To accuse him of attaching any other meaning than that of indefinite

duration to the word, is to accuse him of stultifying himself. But when he writes to describe endless duration he employs other, and less equivocal terms. Alluding to the Pharisees, he says:
"They believe that the wicked are detained in an everlasting prison [*eirgmon aidion*] subject to eternal punishment" [*aidios timoria*]; and the Essenes [another Jewish sect] "allotted to bad souls a dark, tempestuous place, full of never-ceasing punishment [*timoria adialeipton*], where they suffer a deathless punishment, [*athanaton timorian*]."

It is true he sometimes applies *aiónion* to punishment, but this is not his usual custom, and he seems to have done this as one might use the word great to denote eternal duration, that is an indefinite term to describe infinity. But *aidion* and *athanaton* are his favorite terms. These are unequivocal. Were only *aiónion* used to define the Jewish idea of the duration of future punishment, we should have no proof that it was supposed to be endless. *Philo*, who was contemporary with Christ, generally used*aidion* to denote endless, and always used *aiónion* to describe temporary duration. Dr. Mangey, in his edition of Philo, says he never used*aiónion* to interminable duration. He uses the exact phraseology of Matthew, xxv:46, precisely as Christ used it. "It is better not to promise than not to give prompt assistance, for no blame follows in the former case, but in the latter there is dissatisfaction from the weaker class, and a deep hatred and everlasting punishment [*kolasis aiónios*] from such as are more powerful." Here we have the exact terms employed by out Lord, to show that *aiónion* did not mean endless but did mean limited duration in the time of Christ.

Philo always uses *athanaton*, *ateleuteton* or *aidion* to denote endless, and *aiónion* for temporary duration.

Stephens, in his Thesaurus, quotes from a Jewish work, [*Solom. Parab.*] "These they called aiónios, hearing that they had performed the sacred rites for *three entire generations*." This shows conclusively that the expression "three generations" was then one full equivalent of *aiónion*. Now these eminent scholars were Jews who wrote in Greek, and who certainly knew the meaning of the words they employed, and they give to the aionian words the meaning that we are contending for, indefinite duration, to be determined by the subject.

Thus the Jews of our Savior's time avoided using the word *aiónion* to denote endless duration, for applied all through the Bible to temporary affairs, it would not teach it. If Jesus intended to teach the doctrine held by the jews, would he not have used the terms they used? Assuredly; but he did not. He threatened age-lasting, or long-enduring discipline to the believers in endless punishment.*Aiónion* was his word while theirs was *aidion*, *adialeipton*, or *athanaton*, -- thus rejecting their doctrines by not only not employing their phraseology, but by using always and only those words connected with punishment, that denote limited suffering.

And, still further to show that he had no sympathy with those cruel men who procured his death, Jesus said to his disciples: "Take heed and beware of the leaven [doctrine] of the Pharisees and the Sadducees" [believers in endless misery and believers in destruction].

Had *aiónion* been the strongest word, especially had it denoted endless duration, who does not see that it would have been in general use as applied to punishment, by the Jewish Greeks of nineteen centuries ago?

We thus have an unbroken chain of Lexicography, and Classic, Old Testament, and Contemporaneous Usage, all allowing to the word the meaning we claim for it. Indefinite duration is the meaning generally given from the beginning down to the New Testament.

4.-- THE NEW TESTAMENT USAGE.

AION THE SAME IN BOTH TESTAMENTS.

Speaking to those who understood the Old Testament, Jesus and his Apostles employed such words as are used in that book, in the same sense in which they are there used. Not to do so would be to mislead their hearers unless they explained a change of meaning. There is certainly no proof that the word changed its meaning between the Old and New Testaments, accordingly we are under obligation to give it precisely the meaning in the New it had in the Old Testament. This we have seen to be indefinite duration. An examination of the New Testament will show that the meaning is the same, as it should be, in both Testaments.

NUMBER OF TIMES FOUND AND HOW TRANSLATED.

The different forms of the word occur in the New Testament one hundred and ninety-nine times, if I am not mistaken, the noun one hundred and twenty-eight, and the adjective seventy-one times.

Bruder's Concordance, latest edition, gives *aión* one hundred and twenty-six times, and *aiónios* seventy-two times in the New Testament, instead of the former ninety-four, and the latter sixty-six times, as Professor Stuart, following Knapp's Greek text, declares.

In our common translation the noun is rendered seventy-two times ever, twice eternal, thirty-six times world, seven times never, three times evermore, twice worlds, twice ages, once course, once world without end, and twice it is passed over without any word affixed as a translation of it. The adjective is rendered once ever, forty-two times eternal, three times world, twenty-five times everlasting, and once former ages.

1 -- THE KINGDOM OF CHRIST.

Ten times it is applied to the Kingdom of Christ. Luke i:33, "And he shall reign over the house of Jacob forever; and of his kingdom there shall be no end." See also i:55; Heb. vi:20; vii:17,21; I Pet. iv: 11; II Pet. i:11; iii:18; Rev. i:6; xi:15. But the Kingdom of Christ is to end, and he is to surrender all dominion to the Father, therefore endless duration is not taught in these passages. See I Cor. xv.

2 -- THE JEWISH AGE.

It is applied to the Jewish age more than thirty times: 1 Cor. x:11, "Now all these things happened unto them for ensamples; and they are written for our admonition, upon whom the ends of the *world* are come." Consult also Matt. xii:32; xiii:22,39,40,49; xxiv:3; xxviii:20; Mark iv:19; Luke i:70; xvi:8; xx:34; John ix:32; Acts iii:21; xv:18; Rom. xii:2; I Cor. ii:6,7,8; iii:18; II Cor. iv:4; Gal. i:4; Eph. i:21; ii:2; iii:9; 1 Tim. vi:17; II Tim. iv:10; Titus ii:12; Heb. ix:26. But the Jewish age ended with the setting up of the Kingdom of Christ. Therefore the world does not denote endless duration here.

3 -- THE PLURAL FORM. It is used in the plural in Eph. iii:21; "the *age* of the *ages*." *tou aionos ton aionon*. Heb. i:2; xi:3, "By whom he made the worlds." "The worlds were framed by the word of God." There can be but one eternity. To say "By whom he made the eternities" would be to talk nonsense. Endless duration is not inculcated in these texts.

4 -- THE SENSE OF FINITE DURATION.

The word clearly teaches finite duration in such passages as Rom. xvi:25; II Cor. iv:17; II Tim. i:9; Philemon 15; Titus i:2. Read Rom. xvi:25: "Since the *world* (eternity?) began." II Cor. Iv:17: "A far more exceeding *eternal* weight of glory." Here "and" is a word supplied by the translators, and the literal is "an excessively exceeding aionian weight." But endless cannot be exceeded. Therefore *aiónion* does not here mean eternal.

5 --EQUIVALENT TO NOT. The word is used as equivalent to not in Matt. xxi:19; Mark xi:14; John xiii:8; I Cor. viii:13. "Peter said unto him 'thou shalt *never* wash my feet'," is a specimen of this use of the word. It only denotes eternal by accommodation.

6 --APPLIED TO GOD, ETC.

It is applied to God, Christ, the Gospel, the good, the Resurrection world, etc., in which the sense of endless is allowable because imputed to the word by the subject treated, as declared by Taylor and Fuerst, on page 17 of this book, in Rom. i:25; ix:5; xi:36; xvi:27; Gal. i:5; Phil. iv:20; I Tim. i:17; II Tim. iv:18; I John ii:17; I Peter v:11; Rev. vii:12, xv:7; Rom. xvi:26; II Cor. iv:18, v:1; II Tim. ii:10; Heb. vi:2, ix:12,14,15, xiii:20; I Pet. v:10; Rev. iv:10; John viii:35, xii:34, xiv:16; II Cor. ix:9, xi:31; Gal. i:5; Eph. iii:11; II Tim. iv:18; Heb. vii: 24,28, xiii:8,21; I Pet. i:25; II Pet. iii:18; II John 2; Jude 25; Rev. i: 18, iv:9,10, v:13, x:6, xxii:5.

7.--LIFE ETERNAL. It is applied to life, "Everlasting and Eternal Life." But this phrase does not so much denote the duration, as the quality of the Blessed Life. It seems to have the sense of durable in these passages: Matt. xix:16,29, xxv:46; Mark x:17,30; Luke x:25, xvi: 9, xviii:18,30; John iii:15,16,36, iv:14,36, v:24,39, vi: 27,40,47,54,68, x:28, xii:25,50, xvii:2,3; Rom. ii:7, v:21, vi:22,23, Gal. vi:8; II Thess. ii:16; I Tim. i:16, vi:12; Titus i:2, iii:7; Heb. v:9; I John i:2, ii:25, iii:15, v:11,13,20; Jude 21; Mark x:30; Luke xviii:30; John iv:14, vi:51,58, viii:51,52, x:28, xi:26. See this subject treated further on.

PASSAGES DENOTING LIMITED DURATION.

Let us state more definitely several passages in which all will agree that the word cannot have the sense of endless.

Matt. xxii:22, "The care of this *world*, and the deceitfulness of riches, choke the word," the cares of that age or "time." Verses 39, 40,

49, "The harvest is the end of the *world*," *i.e.* age, Jewish age, the same taught in Matt. xxiv, which some who heard Jesus speak were to live to see, and did see. Luke i:33, "And he (Jesus) shall reign over the house of Jacob *for ever*, and of his kingdom there shall be no end." The meaning is, he shall reign to the ages (*eis tous aionas*). That long, indefinite duration is meant here, but limited, is evident from I Cor. xv:28, "And when all things shall be subdued unto him, then shall the Son also himself be subject unto him that put all things under him, that God may be all in all." His reign is for ever, *i.e.*, to the ages, but it is to cease. Luke i:55, "As he spake to our fathers, to Abraham, and to his seed *for ever*, (to an age, *aiónos*.) Luke i:70. "As he spake by the mouth of his holy prophets, which have been since the *world* began," or "from an age," (*ap aiónos*). "Of old," would be the plain construction. Luke xvi:8, "For the children of this*world* are in their generation wiser than the children of light." That is, the people of that time were more prudent in the management of their affairs than were the Christians of that day in their plans. John ix:32, "Since the *world* began was it not heard that any man opened the eyes of one that was born blind." From the age, (*ek tou aiónos*) that is from the beginning of our knowledge and history. Romans xvi:25, "Since the world began," clearly shows a duration less than eternity, inasmuch as the mystery that had been secret since the world began, was then revealed. The mystery was*aiónion* but did not last eternally. It was "now made manifest" "to all nations." Phil. iv:20. "Now unto God and our Father be glory *for ever and ever*," for the ages of the ages (*eis tous aiónas ton aiónon*). (Gal. i:5 same.) "For the eternities of the eternities," is an absurd expression. But ages of ages is a proper sentence. Eternity may be meant here, but if the word *aión* expressed the idea, such a reduplication would be weak and improper. I Tim. vi: 17, "Charge them that are rich in this *world*." (age or time). I Tim. i: 17. "Now to the King *eternal* (of the ages) be glory for the *ages of the ages*." What is this but an asscription of the ages to the God of the ages? Eternity can only be meant here as ages piled on ages imply long, and possibly endless duration. "All the ages are God's; him let the ages glorify," is the full import of the words. Translate the words eternity, and what nonsense. "Now to the God of the eternities (!) Be glory for the eternities of the eternities (!!) Heb. i:8, "The *age of the* *age.*" Eph. ii:7, "That in the *ages* (*aións*) to come he might show the exceeding riches of his grace." Here at least two *aións, eternities* are to come. Certainly one of them must end before the other begins. Eph. iii:21, "The generations of *the age of the ages.*" IITim. iv:18, "*The age of the ages.*" The same form of expression is in Heb. xiii:21; I Pet. iv: 11; Rev. i:6, iv:9, v:13, vii:12, xiv:11, xv:7, xx:10. When we read that the smoke of their torment ascends *eis aiónas aiónon,* for ages of ages, we get the idea of long, indefinite, but limited duration, for as an age is limited, any number however great, must be limited. The moment we say the smoke of their torment goes up for eternities of eternities, we transform the sacred rhetoric in jargon. There is but one eternity, therefore as we read of more than one *aión*, it follows that *aión* cannot mean eternity. Again, I Cor. x:11, "Our admonition, on whom *the*ENDS of the *aións* (ages, *ta tele ton aiónon*) have come." That is, the close of the Mosaic and the beginning of the gospel age. How absurd to "ends of the eternities!" Here the apostle had passed more than one, and entered, consequently, upon at least a third *aión*. Heb. ix:26, "Now at an end of the *ages.*" Matt. xviii:39, 40, xxiv:4, "The conclusion of the *age.*" Eternity has no end. And to say ends of eternities is to talk nonsense. II Tim. ii:9, "Before the *world* began," *i.e.*, before the *aiónion* times began. There was no beginning to eternity, therefore the adjective *aiónion* here has no such meaning as eternal. The fact that *aión* is said to end and begin, is a demonstration that it does not mean eternity.

ABSURDITY OF POPULAR VIEWS.

Translate the word eternity, and how absurd the Bible phraseology becomes! It represent the Bible as saying, "To whom be the glory *during* the ETERNITIES, even TO THE ETERNITIES." Gal. i:5. "Now all these things happened unto them, for ensamples, and they are written for our admonition upon whom *the ends*OF THE ETERNITIES are come." I Cor. x:11. "That in the ETERNITIES coming he might show the exceeding riches of his grace." Eph. ii.7. "The mystery which hath been hid *from the*ETERNITIES*and from the generations.*" Col. i:26. "But now once in the end of the *eternities*, hath he appeared to put away sin by the sacrifice of himself." Heb. ix: 26. "The harvest *is the end of the eternity.*" Matt. xiii:39. "So shall it be *in the end of this eternity.*" Matt. xiii:40. "Tell us when shall these things be, and what the sign of thy coming, and of the end of the eternity." Matt. xxiv:4. But substitute "age" or "ages," and the sense of the Record is preserved.

IT ACQUIRES VARIOUS MEANINGS.

This is seen in many passages. Luke xx: 34, 35. "The children of this world marry, and are given in marriage; but they which shall be accounted worthy to obtain that *world,* ** are equal unto the angels," etc. Here "that world" (*tou aiónos ekeinou*) denotes the eternal world, not because the word *aión intrinsically* means that, but because the resurrection state is the topic of discourse. The words literally mean that age or epoch, but in this instance the immortal world is the subject that defines the word and gives it a unique meaning. So when the word refers to God, it denotes a different duration than when it applies to the Jewish dispensation. That in some of the places referred to the mooted word has the sense of endless, we do not question, but in all such cases it derives that meaning from the subject connected with it.(51)

Let us indicate its varied use. Matt. vi:13 is probably spurious:(52) "Thine is the glory *forever,*" that is through the ages. Here eternity may be implied, but the phrase "forever" literally means "for the ages." Mark iv:19, same as Matt. i:22. Mark x:30. "But he shall receive a hundred fold now in this time, houses, and brethren, and sisters, and mothers, and children, and lands, with persecutions; and in the*world* to come *eternal* life." Literally, in the age to come the life of that age," *i.e.*, gospel, spiritual, Christian life. We have shown that the world to come denotes the Christian dispensation.-Mark xi:;14. "No man eat fruit of thee hereafter *for ever,*" that is "in the age," meaning the period of the tree's existence.-John xii:34. "The people answered him, We have heard out of the law that Christ abideth *for ever;*" (to the age). The Jews believed that their dispensation was to continue, and Messiah would remain as long as it would last. This language means that Christ was to remain through the Mosaic epoch. So the Jews thought.-John xiii:8. "Thou shalt *never* wash my feet" is equivalent to "Thou shalt not wash my feet."-John xiv:16. "And I will pray the Father and he shall give you another Comforter, that he may abide with you *for ever,*"*eis ton aióna,* "unto the age," that is, accompany them into the coming or Christian era.-John vi:51. 58, "If any man eat of this bread he shall live *for ever*;" *eis ton aióna*, into the age, that is, enjoy the life of the world that is to come, the Christian life. Its duration is not described here at all.-John viii:35. "And the servant abideth not in the house *for ever*; (to the age,) *but* the Son abideth ever."- The Jews are here told that their religion is to be superseded by the Christ only. They are to leave the house because slaves to sin, while the Son will remain to the age-permanently.-John viii:51, 52. "Verily, verily, I say unto you, If a man keep my saying he shall *never* see death. Then said the Jews unto him, Now we know that thou hast a devil. Abraham is dead, and the prophets; and thou sayest, If a man keep my saying he shall *never* taste of death." Moral, spiritual death is impossible to a man as long as he keeps the saying of Christ, is the full meaning of the words.

OCCURRENCE OF THE ADJECTIVE.

The adjective *aiónios* is (incorrectly) said by Professor Stuart to[53] occur sixty-six times in the New Testament, be we make it seventy-two times. Of these fifty-seven are used in relation to the happiness of the righteous; three in relation to God or his glory; four are of a miscellaneous nature; and seven relate to the subject of punishment. Now these fifty-seven denote indefinite duration, "everlasting life" being a life that may or may not -- certainly does not always -- endure forever.

Thus the great preponderance of usage in the New Testament is indefinite duration. But if the preponderance were against this usage, we ought, in order to vindicate God's character, to understand it in the sense of limited when describing a Father's punishment of his children.

APPLIED TO PUNISHMENT.

How many times does the word in all its forms describe punishment? Only fourteen times in thirteen passages in the entire New Testament, and these were uttered on ten occasions only. *The Noun,* Matt. xii:32, Mark iii:29, 2 Pet. ii:17, Jude 13, Rev. xiv:11, xix: 3, xx:10. *The Adjective*, Matt. xviii:8, xxv:41, 46, Mark iii:29, 2 Thess. i:9, Jude 7, Heb. vi:2.

Now if God's punishments are limited, we can understand how this word should be used only fourteen times to define them. But if they are endless how can we explain the employment of this equivocal word only fourteen times in the entire New Testament? A doctrine that, if true, ought to crowd every sentence, frown in every line, only stated fourteen times, and that, too, by a word whose uniform meaning everywhere else is limited duration! The idea is preposterous. Such reticence is incredible. If the word denotes limited duration, the punishments threatened in the New Testament are like those that experience teaches follow transgression. But if it means endless, how can we account for the fact that neither Luke nor John records one instance of its use by the Savior, and Matthew but four, and Mark but two, and Paul employs it but twice in his ministry, while John and James in their epistles never allude to it? Such silence is an unanswerable refutation of all attempts to foist the meaning of endless into the word. "Everlasting fire" occurs only three times, "everlasting punishment" only once, and "eternal damnation" once only. Shall any one dare suppose that the New Testament reveals endless torment, and that out of one hundred and ninety-nine occurrences of the word *aion* it is applied to punishment so seldom, and that so many of those who wrote the New Testament never use the word at all? No. The New Testament usage agrees with the meaning in the Greek classics, and in the Old Testament. Does it not strike the candid mind as impossible that God should have concealed this doctrine for thousands of years, and that for forty centuries of revelation he continually employed to teach limited duration the identical word that he at length stretched into the signification of endless duration? The word means limited duration all through the Old Testament; it never had the meaning of endless duration among those who spoke the language, (as we have demonstrated,) but Jesus announced the doctrine of endless punishment, and selected as the Greek word to convey his meaning the very word that in the Classics and the Septuagint never contained any such thought, when there were several words in the copious Greek tongue that unequivocally conveyed the idea of interminable duration! Even if Matthew wrote in Hebrew or in Syro-Chaldaic, he gave a Greek version of his gospel, and in that rejected every word that carries the meaning of endlessness, and appropriated the one which taught nothing of the kind. If this were the blunder of an incompetent translator, or the imperfect record of a reckless scribe, we could understand it, but to say that the inspired pen of the evangelist has deliberately or carelessly jeoparded the immortal welfare of countless millions by employing a word to teach the doctrine of ceaseless woe that up to that very hour taught only limited duration, is to make a declaration that carries its own refutation.

We come now to the sheet-anchor of the great heresy of the partialist church,

THE PRINCIPAL PROOF-TEXT

of an error hoary with antiquity, and not yet wholly abandoned. Matt. xxv:46, is the great proof-text of the doctrine of endless punishment: "These shall go away into everlasting punishment, and the righteous into life eternal." We shall endeavor to establish the following points against the erroneous view of this Scripture. 1. The punishment is not for unbelief, but for not benefitting the needy. 2. The general antecedent usage of the word denoting duration here, in the Classics and in the Old Testament, proves that the duration is limited. 3. One object of punishment being to improve the punished, the punishment here*must* be limited; 4. The events here described took place in this world, and must therefore be of limited duration. 5. The Greek word *kolasin*, rendered punishment, should be rendered chastisement, as reformation is implied in its meaning.

1. THE AIONIAN PUNISHMENT IS FOR EVIL WORKS.

Practical benevolence is the virtue whose reward is here announced, and unkindness is the vice whose punishment is here threatened, and not faith and unbelief, on which heaven and hell are popularly predicated. Matt. xxv:34-45. "Then shall the King say unto them on his right hand, Come, ye blessed of my Father, inherit the kingdom prepared for you from the foundation of the world: For I was a hungered, and ye game me meat: I was thirsty, and ye gave me drink: I was a stranger and ye took me in: Naked, and ye clothed me; I was sick, and ye visited me: I was in prison, and ye came unto me. Then shall the righteous answer him, saying, Lord, when saw we thee a hungered, and fed thee? or thirsty, and gave thee drink? When saw we thee a stranger and took thee in? or naked, and clothed thee? Or when saw we thee sick, or in prison, and came unto thee? And the King shall answer and say unto them, Verily I say unto you,*Inasmuch as ye have done it unto one of the least of these my brethren, ye have done it unto me.* Then shall he say unto them on the left hand, Depart from me, ye cursed, into everlasting fire, prepared for the devil and his angels: For I was a hungered, and ye gave me no meat: I was thirsty, and ye gave me no drink: I was a stranger, and ye took me not in: naked and ye clothed me not: sick, and in prison, and ye visited me not. Then shall they also answer him, saying, Lord, when saw we thee a hungered, or athirst, or a stranger, or naked, or sick, or in prison, and did not minister unto thee? Then shall he answer them, saying, Verily I say unto you, *Inasmuch as ye did it not to one of the least of these, ye did it not to me.*"

If cruelty to the poor --neglect of them even,--constitutes rejection of Christ --as is plainly taught here --and all who are guilty are to suffer endless torment "who then can be saved?" the single consideration that works, and not faith are here made the test of discipleship, cuts away the foundation of the popular view of this text.

2. THE WORD AIONION DENOTES LIMITED DURATION.

This appears in Classic and Old Testament usage. It is impossible that Jesus should have used the word rendered everlasting in a different sense than we have shown to have been its meaning in antecedent literature.

3. GOD'S PUNISHMENTS ARE REMEDIAL.

All God's punishments are those of a Father, and must therefore be adapted to the improvement of his children. Heb. xii:5, "My son, despise not thou the chastening of the Lord, nor faint when thou art rebuked of him: For whom the Lord loveth he chasteneth, and scourgeth every son whom he receiveth. If ye endure chastening, God dealeth with you as with sons: for what son is he whom the father chasteneth not? Furthermore, we have had fathers of our flesh which corrected us, and we gave them reverence. Shall we not much rather be in subjection to the Father of spirits, and live? For they verily for a few days chastened us after their own pleasure; but *he for our profit* that we might be partakers of his holiness. Now no chastening for the present seemeth to be joyous, but grievous; nevertheless, *afterward it yieldeth the peaceable fruit of righteousness unto them which are exercised thereby.*" Prov. iii:11, 12. "My son, despise not the hastening of the Lord; neither be weary of his correction: For whom the Lord loveth he correcteth; even as a father the son in whom he delighteth." Lam. iii:31, 33. "For the Lord will not cast off forever: But though he cause grief, yet will he have compassion according to the multitude of his mercies. For he doth not afflict willingly, nor grieve the children of men." See also Job v, xxv; Lev. xxvi; Psalms cxxix:67, 71, 75; Jer. ii:19.

4. THESE EVENTS HAVE OCCURRED.

The events here described too place in this world within thirty years of the time when Jesus spoke. They are now past. In Matt. xxiv:4, the disciples asked our Lord when the then existing age would end. The word (*aión*) is unfortunately translated world. Had he meant world he would have employed*kosmos*, which means world, as *aión* does not. After describing the particulars he announced that they would all be fulfilled, and the *aión* end in that generation, before some of his auditors should die. If he was correct the end came then. And this is demonstrated by a careful study of the entire discourse, running through Matthew xxiv and xxv. The disciples asked Jesus how they should know his coming and the *end* of the *age*. They did not inquire concerning the end of the actual world, as it is incorrectly translated, but age. This question Jesus answered by describing the signs so that they, his questioners, the disciples themselves, might perceive the approach of the end of the Jewish dispensation (*aión*). He speaks fifteen times in the discourse of his speedy coming, (Matt. xxiv:3, 27, 30, 37, 39, 42, 46, 48, 50, and xxv:6, 10, 13, 19, 27, 31). He addresses those who shall be alive at his coming. Matt. xxiv:6. "*Ye* shall hear of wars, etc." 20. "Pray that *your* flight be not in the winter." 33, 34. "So likewise*ye* when *ye* shall see all these things, know that it is near, *even* at the doors. Verily I say unto you, *This generation shall not pass, till all these things be fulfilled.*"

Campbell, Clarke, Wakefield, and Newton(54) translate the phrase, end of the world (*sunteleia tou aiónos*) "conclusion of the age," "end of this dispensation." The question was, then, what shall indicate thy second coming and the end of the Mosaic economy (*aión*)? "When shall all these things be fulfilled?" Mark xiii:1, 34. He spoke of the temple (Luke xxi:5, 7,) saying one stone should not be left on another, and the question of his disciples was, how shall we know when this is to take place? The answer is, "*Ye* shall hear of wars." xxiv: 6. "*Ye* shall see the abomination of desolation." 15. "Pray that *your* flight be not in winter." 20. The adverbs "Then" and "When" connect all the events related in the two chapters in one unbroken series. And what infallible token did he give that these events would occur "then?" Matt. xxiv:34. "Verily I say unto you this generation shall not pass till*all* these things be fulfilled." What things? The "son of man coming in his glory in the clouds," and the end of the existing *aión*, or age. Mark phrases it: "This generation shall not pass till all these things be done." See Luke xxi:25, 32. This whole account is a parable describing the end of the Jewish *aión*, age, or economy, signalized by the destruction of Jerusalem, and the establishment if the new *aión*, world, or age to come, that is the Christian dispensation. Now on the authority of Jesus himself the *aión* then existing ended within a generation, namely, about A.D. 70. Hence those who were sent away into *aiónion* punishment, or the punishment of that *aión*, were sent into a condition corresponding in duration to the meaning of the word *aión*, i.e., age-lasting. A punishment cannot be endless, when defined by an adjective derived from a noun describing an event, the end of which is distinctly stated to have come.

5. THE WORD TRANSLATED PUNISHMENT MEANS IMPROVEMENT.

The word is *Kolasin*. It is thus authoritavely defined: *Greenfield*, "Chastisement, punishment." *Hedericus*, "The trimming of the luzuriant branches of a tree or vine to improve it and make it fruitful."*Donnegan*, "The act of clipping or pruning --restriction, restraint, reproof, check, chastisement." *Grotius*, "The kind of punishment which tends to the improvement of the criminal, is what the Greek philosophers called *kolasis* or chastisement." *Liddell*, "Pruning, checking, punishment, chastisement, correction." *Max Muller*, "Do we want to know what was uppermost in the minds of those who formed the word for punishment, the Latin *pœna* or *punio*, to punish, the root *pu* in Sanscrit, which means to *cleanse*, to *purify*, tells us that the Latin derivation was originally formed, not to express mere striking or torture, but cleansing, correcting, delivering from the stain of sin." That it had this meaning in Greek usage we cite Plato: (55) "For the natural or accidental evils of others, no one gets angry, or admonishes, or teaches or punishes (kolazei) them, but we pity those afflicted with such misfortunes. ** For if, O Socrates, you will consider what is the design of punishing (kolazein) the wicked, this of itself will show you that men think virtue something that may be acquired; for no one punishes (*kolazei*) the wicked, looking to the past only, simply for the wrong he has done,--that is, *no one does this thing who does not act*LIKE A WILD BEAST, desiring only revenge, without thought --hence he who seeks to punish (*kolazein*) *with reason*, does not punish for the sake of the past wrong deed, ** but for the sake of the future, that neither the man himself who is punished, may do wrong again, nor any other who has seen him chastised. And he who entertains this thought, must believe that virtue may be taught, and *he punishes* (*kolazei*) *for the purpose of deterring from wickedness*." Like many other words this is not always used in its exact and full sense. The apocrypha employs it as the synonym of suffering, regardless of reformation. See Wis. iii:11, xvi:1; I Mac. vii:7. See also Josephus.(56) It is found but four times in the New Testament. Acts iv: 21, the Jews let John and Peter go, "finding nothing further how they might punish them" (*kolazo*). Did they not aim to reform them? Was not their punishment to cause them to return to the Jewish fold? From their standpoint the word was certainly used to convey the idea of reformation. 1 John iv:18. "Fear hath*torment*." Here the word "torment" should be *restraint*. It is thus translated in the Emphatic Diaglot. The idea is, if we have perfect love we do not fear God, but if we fear we are restrained from loving him. "Fear hath restraint." The word is used here with but one of its meanings. In 2 Peter ii:9, the apostle uses the word as our Lord did: the unjust are reserved unto the day of judgement to be punished (*kolazomenous*). This accords exactly with the lexicography of the word, and the general usage in the Bible and in Greek literature agrees with the meaning given by the lexicographers. Now, though the word rendered punishment is sometimes used to signify suffering alone, by Josephus and others, surely Divine inspiration will use it in its exact sense. We must therefore be certain that in the New Testament, when used by Jesus to designate divine punishment, it is generally used with its full meaning. The lexicographers and Plato, above, show us what that is, suffering, restraint, followed by correction, improvement.

From this meaning of the word, torment is by no means excluded. God does indeed torment his children when they go astray. He is a "consuming fire," and burns with terrible severity towards us when we sin, but it is not because he hates but because he loves us. He is a refiner's fire tormenting the immortal gold of humanity in the crucible of punishment, until the dross of sin is purged away. Mal. ii: 2,3, "But who may abide the day of his coming? and who shall stand when he appeareth? for he is like a *refiner's fire* and like fuller's soap. And he shall sit as a refiner and purifier of silver: and he shall *purify* the sons of Levi, and purge them as gold or silver, that *they may offer unto the Lord an offering in righteousness*." Therefore *kolasis* is just the word to describe his punishments. They do for the soul what pruning does for the tree, what the crucible of the refiner does for the silver ore.

Even if *aiónion* and *kolasis* were both of doubtful signification, and were we only uncertain as to their meaning we ought to *give God the benefit of the doubt* and understand the word in a way to honor him, that is, in a limited sense, but when all but universal usage ascribes to *aiónion* limited duration, and the word *kolasin* is declared by all authorities to mean pruning, discipline, it is astonishing that a Christian teacher should be found to *imagine* that when both words are together, they can mean anything else than temporary punishment ending in reformation, especially in a discourse in which it is expressly declared that the complete fulfillment was in this life, and within a generation of the time when the prediction was uttered.

Therefore, (1) the fulfillment of the language in this life, (2) the meaning of *aiónion*, (3) and the meaning of *kolasis*, demonstrate that the penalty threatened in Matt. xxv:46, is a limited one. It is a threefold cord that human skill cannot break. Prof. Tayler Lewis thus translates Matt. xxv:46. "These shall go away into the punishment (the restraint, imprisonment,) of the world to come, and those into the life of the world to come." And he says "*that is all that we can etymologically or exegetically make of the word in this passage*."

Hence, also, the *zoen aiónion* (life eternal) is not endless, but is a condition resulting from a good character. The intent of the phrase is not to teach immortal happiness, nor does *kolasin aiónion* indicate endless punishment. Both phrases, regardless of duration refer to the limited results wronging or blessing others, extending possibly through Messiah's reign until "the end" (1 Cor. xv.). Both describe consequences of conduct to befall those consequences antedate the immortal state.

A COMMON OBJECTION NOTICED.

"Then eternal life is not endless, for the same Greek adjective qualifies life and punishment." This does not follow, for the word is used in Greek in different senses in the same sentence; as Hab. iii:6. "And the *everlasting* mountains were scattered --his ways are *everlasting*." Suppose we apply the popular argument here. The mountains and God must be of equal duration, for the same word is applied to both. Both are temporal or both are endless. But the mountains are expressly stated to be temporal --they "were scattered," --therefore God is not eternal. Or God is eternal and therefore the mountains must be. But they cannot be, for they were scattered. The argument does not hold water. The *aiónion* mountains are all to be destroyed. Hence*the word may denote both limited and unlimited duration in the same passage, the different meanings to be determined by the subject treated.*

But it may be said that this phrase "everlasting" or "eternal life" does not usually denote endless existence, but the life of the gospel, spiritual life, the Christian life, regardless of its duration. In more than fifty of the seventy-two times that the adjective occurs in the New Testament, it describes life. What is eternal life? Let the Scriptures answer. John iii:36, "He that believeth on the Son hath everlasting life." John v:24, "He that believeth on him that sent me hath everlasting life, and shall not come into condemnation, but IS PASSED from death unto life." John vi:47, "He that believeth on me hath everlasting life." So verse 54. John xvii:3, "THIS IS LIFE ETERNAL*to know thee*, the only true God, and Jesus Christ whom thou hast sent." Eternal life is the life of the gospel. Its duration depends on the possessor's fidelity. It is no less the *aiónion* life, if one abandon it in a month after acquiring it. It consists in knowing, loving and serving God. It is the Christian life, regardless of its duration. How often the good fall from grace. Believing, they have the *aiónion* life, but they lose it by apostasy. Notoriously it is not, in thousands of cases, endless. The life is of an indefinite length, so that the usage of the adjective in the New Testament is altogether in favor of giving the word the sense of limited duration. Hence Jesus does not say "he that believeth shall enjoy endless happiness," but "he*hath* everlasting life," and "*is passed* from death unto life."

It scarcely need here be proved that the *aiónion* life can be acquired and lost. Heb. vi:4, "For it is impossible for those who were once enlightened, and have tasted of the heavenly gift, and were made partakers of the holy Ghost, and have tasted the good word of God, and the powers of the world to come, if they shall fall away, to renew them again unto repentance: seeing they crucify to themselves the Son of God afresh, and put him to an open shame." A life that can thus be lost is not intrinsically endless.

That the adjective is thus consistently used to denote indefinite duration will appear from several illustrations, some of which we have already given. 2 Cor. iv:17, "A far more exceeding and *eternal* weight of glory," or, as the original reads, "exceeding an *aiónion* weight of glory excessively." Now eternal, endless cannot be exceeded, but *aiónion* can be, therefore *aiónion* is not eternal. Again, Rev. xiv:6, "The*everlasting* gospel." The gospel is good news. When all shall have learned its truths it will no longer be news. There will be no such thing as gospel extant. Faith will be fruition, hope lost in sight, and the *aiónion* gospel, like the *aiónion* covenant of the elder dispensation, will be abrogated, not destroyed, but fulfilled and passed away. Again, 2 Pet. i:11, "The *everlasting* kingdom of our Lord and Savior Jesus Christ." This kingdom is to be dissolved. Jesus is to surrender his dominion. 1 Cor. xv:24, "Then cometh the end, when he shall have delivered up the kingdom to God even the Father," etc. The everlasting kingdom of Christ will end.

The word may mean endless when applied to life, and not when applied to punishment, even in the same sentence, though we think duration is not considered so much as the intensity of joy or the sorrow in either case.

WORDS TEACHING ENDLESS DURATION.

But the Blessed Life has not been left dependent on so equivocal a word. The soul's immortal and happy existence is taught in the New Testament, by words that in the Bible are never applied to anything that is of limited duration. They are applied to God and the soul's happy existence only. These words are *akataluton*, imperishable; *amarantos* and *amarantinos*, unfading; *aphtharto*, immortal, incorruptible; and *athanasian*, immortality. Let us quote some of the passages in which these words occur:

Heb. vii:15, 16, "And it is yet far more evident: for that after the similitude of Melchizedek there ariseth another priest, who is made, not after the law of a carnal commandment, but after the power of an *endless* (*akatalutos*, imperishable) life." 1 Pet. i:3, 4, "Blessed be the God and Father of our Lord Jesus Christ, which according to his abundant mercy, hath begotten us again unto a lively hope by the resurrection of Jesus Christ from the dead, to an inheritance *incorruptible*, (*aphtharton*,) and undefiled, and that *fadeth not* (*amaranton*) away." 1 Pet. v:4, "And when the chief Shepherd shall appear, ye shall receive a crown of glory that*fadeth not* (*amarantinos*) away." 1 Tim. i:17, "Now unto the King eternal, *immortal*, (*aphtharto*,) invisible, the only wise god, be honor and glory forever and ever, Amen." Rom. i:23, "And changed the glory of the *incorruptible* God into an image made like to corruptible man." 1 Cor. ix:25, "Now they do it to obtain a corruptible crown; but we an *incorruptible*." 1 Cor. xv:51-54, "Behold, I shew you a mystery; We shall not all sleep, but we shall be changed, in a moment, in the twinkling of an eye, at the last trump: for the trumpet shall sound, and the dead shall be raised *incorruptible*, (*aphthartoi*,) and we shall be changed. For this corruptible must put on *incorruption*, (*aphtharsian*,) and this mortal must put on *immortality* (*athanasian*). So when this corruptible shall have put on *incorruption*, (*aphtharsian*,) and this mortal shall have put on *immortality*, (*athanasian*,) then shall be brought to pass the saying that is written, Death is swallowed up in victory." Rom. ii:7, "To them who by patient continuance in well doing seek for glory and honor and *immortality*, (*aphtharsia*,) eternal life." 1 Cor. xv:42, "So also is the resurrection of the dead. It is sown in corruption, it is raised in *incorruption* (*aphtharsia*)." See also verse 50, 2 Tim i:10, "Who brought life and *immortality* (*aphtharsian*) to light, through the gospel." 1 Tim. vi:16, "Who only hath *immortality* (*athanasian*)."

Now these words are applied to God and the soul's happiness. They are words that in the Bible are never applied to punishment, or to anything perishable. They would have been affixed to punishment had the Bible intended to teach endless punishment. And certainly they show the error of those who declare that the indefinite word *aiónion* is all the word, or the strongest word in the Bible declarative of the endlessness of the life beyond the grave. A little more study of the subject would prevent such reckless statements and would show that the happy, endless life does not depend at all on the pet word of the partialist critics.

THOMAS DE QUINCEY'S VIEWS.

It will be of interest to give here the views of Thomas De Quincey, one of the most accurate students of language, and profoundest reasoners and thinkers among English scholars. He states the facts of the case with almost perfect accuracy: "I used to be annoyed and irritated by the false interpretation given to the Greek word *aión*, and given necessarily, therefore, to the Greek adjective *aiónios* as its immediate derivative. It was not so much the falsehood of this interpretation, as the narrowness of that falsehood that disturbed me. . . . . That reason which gives to this word *aiónion* what I do not scruple to call a *dreadful* importance, is the same reason, and no other, which prompted the dishonesty concerned in the ordinary interpretation of this word. The word happened to connect itself --but *that* was no practical concern of mine, --me it had not biased in the one direction, nor should it have biased any just critic in the counter direction --happened, I say, to connect itself with the ancient dispute upon the *duration* of future punishment. What was meant by the *aiónion* punishments of the next world? Was the proper sense of the word *eternal*, or was it not? . . . That argument runs thus --that the ordinary construction of the word *aiónion*, as equivalent to everlasting, could not possibly be given up, when associated with penal misery, because in that case, and by the very same act, the idea of eternity must be abandoned as applicable to the counter bliss of paradise. Torment and blessedness, it was argued, punishment and beatification stood upon the same level; the same word it was, the word *aiónion*, which qualified the duration of either; and if eternity, in the most rigorous acceptation, fell away from the one idea, it must equally fall away from the other. Well, be it so. But that would not settle the question. It might be very painful to renounce a long cherished anticipation, but the necessity of doing so could not be received as a sufficient reason for adhering to the old unconditional use of the word*aiónion*. The argument is --that we must retain the old sense of eternal, because else we lose upon one scale what we had gained upon the other. But what then? would be the reasonable man's retort. We are not to accept or to reject a new construction (if otherwise the more colorable,) of the word *aiónion*, simply because the consequences might seem such, as, upon the whole, to displease us. We may gain nothing; for by the new interpretation our loss may balance our gain, and we may prefer the old arrangement. But how monstrous is all this! We are not summoned as to a choice of two different arrangements that may suit different tastes, but to a grave question as to what is the sense and operation of the word *aiónion*. . . . Meantime all this speculation, first and last, is pure nonsense. *Aiónian* does not mean eternal, neither does it mean of limited duration. Nor would the unsettling of *aiónian* in its old use, as applied to punishment, to torment, to misery, etc., carry with it any necessary unsettling of the idea in its application to the beatitudes of Paradise.

What is an *aión*? The duration or cycle of existence which belongs to any object, not individually of itself, but universally, in right of its genius. . . . Man has a certain *aiónian* life; possibly ranging somewhere about the period of seventy years assigned in the Psalms. . . . The period would in that case represent the "*aión*" of the individual Tellurian; but the "*aión*" of the Tellurian race would probably amount to many millions of our earthly years, and it would remain an unfathomable mystery, deriving no light at all from the septuagenarian "*aión*" of the individual; though between the two *aións* I have no doubt that some secret link of connection does and must subsist, however undiscoverable by human sagacity. . . .

This only is discoverable, as a general tendency, that the *aión*, or generic period of evil is constantly towards a fugitive duration. The *aión*, it is alleged, must always express the same idea, whatever that may be; if it is less than eternity for the evil cases, then it must be less for the good ones. Doubtless the idea of an *aión* is in one sense always uniform, always the same, --viz., as a tenth or a twelfth is always the same. Arithmetic could not exist if any caprice or variation affected their ideas --a tenth is always more than an eleventh, always less than a ninth. But this uniformity of ratio and proportion does not hinder but that a tenth may now represent a guinea, and the next moment represent a thousand guineas. *The exact amount of the duration expressed by an aión depends altogether upon the particular subject which yields the aión.* It is, as I have said, a radix, and like an algebraic square-root or cube-root, though governed by the most rigorous laws of limitation, it must vary in obedience to the nature of the particular subject whose radix it forms." De Quincey's conclusions are:

A. That man who allows himself to infer the eternity of evil from the counter eternity of good, builds upon the mistake of assigning a stationary and mechanic value to the idea of an *aión*, whereas the very purpose of Scripture in using the word was to evade such a value. *The word is always varying for the very purpose of keeping if faithful to a spiritual identity.* The period or duration of every object would be an essentially variable quantity, were it not mysteriously commensurate to the inner nature of that object as laid open to the eyes of God. And thus it happens, that *everything in the world* possibly without a solitary exception, *has its own separate aión; how many entities, so many aións.*

B. But if it be an excess of blindness which can overlook the *aiónian* differences amongst even neutral entities, much deeper is that blindness which overlooks the separate tendencies of things evil and things good. Naturally, all evil is fugitive and allied to death.

C. I, separately, speaking for myself only, profoundly believe that the Scriptures ascribe absolute and metaphysical eternity to one sole being --viz., God; and derivatively to all others according to the interest which they can plead in God's favor. Having anchorage in God, innumerable entities may possibly be admitted to a participation in divine *aión*. But what interest in the favor of God can belong to falsehood, to malignity, to impurity? To invest *them* with *aiónian* privileges, is, in effect, and by its results, to distrust and to insult the Deity. Evil would *not* be evil, if it had that power of self-subsistence which is imparted to it in supposing its *aiónian* life to be co-eternal with that which crowns and glorifies the good."(57)

REV. E. H. SEARS.

Says Edmund H. Sears: "The passage has often been regarded as if the chief thing to be considered was the duration of the punishment of the unrighteous, over against the duration of the life of the righteous, and that since both are described by the same word, they are of like duration. That would undoubtedly be so if mere duration or extension by time were expressed at all, or any way involved in the contrast. But that, as I should interpret, is not the meaning of the original word. The element of time, as we measure things, does not enter into it at all. Not duration, but quality[editor's emphasis], is the chief thing involved in this word rendered 'eternal.' . . The word *aión* and its derivatives, rendered 'eternal' and 'everlasting,' describe an economy complete in itself, and the duration must depend on the nature of the economy. . . . The New Testament, if it reveals anything, reveals the *aión* --the dispensation that lies next to this, and gathers into it the momentous results of our probation in time. But what lies beyond *that* in the cycles of a coming eternity, I do not believe has been revealed to the highest angel. Think of that endless Beyond! If every atom of the globe were counted off, and every atom stood for a million years, still we have not apporached a conception of endless duration. And yet sinful and fallible men affirm that their fellow sinners are to be given over to indescribable agonies through those millions of years thus repeated, and even then the clocks of eternity have only struck the morning hour! that the hells of pent-up anguish are to streak eternity with blood in lines parallel forever with the being of God! If Gabriel should come and tell us that we should have a right to believe that the history of the infinite future infolded in the bosom of God, had not been given to Gabriel!"(58)

DID JESUS EMPLOY THE POPULAR PHRASEOLOGY?

It is often remarked that as, according to Josephus, the Jews in our Savior's times believed in endless punishment, Jesus must have taught the same doctrine, as "he employed the terms the Jews used." But this is not true, as we have shown. Christ and his apostles did not employ the phraseology that the Jews used to describe this doctrine. As we have shown Philo used *athanaton* and *ateleuteton* meaning immortal, and interminable. He says,(59)*zoe apothneskonta aeikai tropon tina thanaton athanaton upomeinon kai ateleuteton*, "to live always dying, and to undergo an immortal and interminable death." He also employs *aidion*, but not *aiónion.*(60) Josephus says: "They, the Pharisees, believe 'the souls of the bad are allotted *aidios eirgmos, to an eternal prison*, and punished with *adialeiptos timoria, eternal retribution.*" In describing the doctrine of the Essenes, Josephus says they believe "the souls of the bad are sent to a dark and tempestuous cavern, full of *adialeiptos timoria, incessant punishment.*" But the phraseology of Jesus and the apostles *olethros aiónios* or *aióniou kriseos* "eternal chastisement," or "eternal condemnation." The Jews contemporary with Jesus call retribution *aidios*, or *adialeiptos timoria*, while the Savior calls it *aiónios krisis*, or *kolasis aiónios*, and the apostles *olethros aiónios, everlasting destruction*; and *puros aiónios, eternal fire*. Had Jesus and his apostles used the terms employed by the Jews to whom they spake, we should be compelled to admit that they taught the popular doctrine. See this point further elucidated at the end of this volume on the word *Aidios*.

"To live always dying and undergo an endless death," is the language of "orthodox" pulpits, and of the Greek Jews, but our Savior and his apostles carefully avoided such horrible blasphemy as to charge God with being the author of so diabolical a cruelty.

Says a learned scholar:[(61)] "*Aiónios* is a word of sparing occurrence among ancient classical Greek writers; nor is it by any means the common term employed by them to signify*eternal.* On the contrary, they much more frequently make use of *aidios, aei ón*, or some similar mode of speech, for this purpose. . . . To me it appears that the Seventy, by choosing *aiónios* to represent *olam*, testify that they did not understand the Hebrew word to signify *eternal.* Had they so understood it, they would certainly have translated it by some more decisive word; some term, which, like *aidios* is more commonly employed in Greek, to signify that which has neither beginning no end."

Let us now allude to the other texts in the New Testament in which the word is applied to punishment.

"NEVER FORGIVENESS --ETERNAL DAMNATION."

Matt. xii:32. "Whosoever speaketh against the Holy Ghost, it shall not be forgiven him, neither in this *world*, neither in the world to come." Parallel passages: Mark iii:29. "But he that shall blaspheme against the Holy Ghost hath never (*aióna*) forgiveness, but is in danger of eternal (*aiónion*) damnation." Luke xii:10. "And whosoever shall speak a word against the Son of man, it shall be forgiven him; but unto him that blasphemeth against the Holy Ghost it shall not be forgiven." Literally, "neither in this age nor the coming," that is, neither in the Mosaic, nor the Christian age or dispensation. but then, these ages will both end, and in the dispensation of the fullness of times, or ages, all are to be redeemed, (Eph. i:10.) Mark iii:29 is the same as Matt. xii:32. The Greek differs slightly, and is rendered literally, "has not forgiveness to the age, but is liable to age-lasting judgment." The thought of the Savior is, that those who should attribute his good deeds to an evil spirit would be so hardened that his religion would have difficulty in affecting them. Endless damnation is not thought of, and cannot be extorted from the language.

In the New Testament the "end of the age," and "ages" is a common expression, referring to what has now passed. See Col. i:26, Heb. ix: 26, Matt. xiii:39, 40, 49, xxiv:3. Says Locke(62) "The nation of the Jews were the kingdom and people God whilst the law stood. And this kingdom of God, under the Mosaic constitution was called *aión outos,* this age, or as it is commonly translated, this world. But the kingdom of God was to be under the Messiah, wherein the economy and constitution of the Jewish church, and the nation itself, that in opposition to Christ adhered to it, was to be laid aside, is in the New Testament called *aión mellon*, the world or age to come."

Another writer(63) adds: "Why the times under the law, were called *kronoi aiónioi*, we may find reason in their jubilees, which were *aiónes*, "secula," or "ages," by which all the time under the law, was measured; and so *kronoi aiónioi*; is used, 2 Tim. i:9. Tit. i:2. And so *aiónes* are put for the times of the law, or the jubilees, Luke i:70, Acts iii:21, 1 Cor. ii:7, x:11, Eph. iii:9, Col. i:26, Heb. ix:26. And so God is called the rock of *aiónon*, of ages, Isa. xxvi:4, in the same sense that he is called the rock of Israel, Isa. xxx:29, i. e. the strength and support of the Jewish state;-- for it is of the Jews the prophet here speaks. So Exod. xxi:6, *eis ton aióna* signifies not as we translate it, "forever," but "to the jubilee;" which will appear if we compare Lev. xxv:39-41, and Exod. xxi:2."

Pearce(64) in his commentary, says "Rather, neither in this age, nor in the age to come: i. e., neither in this age when the law of Moses subsists, nor in that also, when the kingdom of heaven, which is at hand, shall succeed to it. The Greek *aión*, seems to signify age here, as it often does in the New Testament, (see chap. xiii:40; xxiv:3; Col. i: 26; Eph. iii:5, 21.) and according to its most proper signification. If this be so, then this age means the Jewish one, the age while their law subsisted and was in force; and the age to come (see Heb. vi:5; Eph. ii:7.) means that under the Christian dispensation."

Wakefield observes:[(65)] "Age, *aióni; i. e.*, the Jewish dispensation which was then in being, or the Christian, which was going to be."

Clarke:[(66)] "Though I follow the common translation, (Matt. xii:31, 32.) yet I am fully satisfied the meaning of the words is, neither in this dispensation, viz., the Jewish, nor in that which is to come, the Christian. *Olam ha-bo*, the world to come, is a constant phrase for the times of the Messiah, in the Jewish writers." See also Hammond, Rosenmuller, etc.,[(67)]. Take Hebrews ix:26, as an example. "For then must he (Christ) often have suffered since the foundation of the world (*kosmos*, literal world) but now once *in the end of the world* (*aiónon*, age) hath he appeared to put away sin by the sacrifice of himself." What world was at its end when Christ appeared? Indubitably the Jewish age. The world or age to come (*aión*) must be the Christian dispensation, as in 1 Cor. x:11, where Paul says that upon him and his contemporaries "the ends of the world are come."

These passages state in strong language the heinous nature of the sin referred to. The age or world to come is not beyond the grave, but it is the Christian dispensation. It had a beginning eighteen centuries ago, and it will end when Jesus delivers the kingdom to God, the Father. (1 Cor. xv).

EVERLASTING FIRE.

Matt. xviii:8. "Wherefore if thy hand or thy foot offend thee, cut them off, and cast them from thee: it is better for thee to enter into life halt or maimed, rather than having two hands, or two feet, to be cast into everlasting fire." Matt. xxv:41 uses the same phraseology. "The *everlasting* fire, prepared for the Devil and his angels." Also Jude 7. "Even as Sodom and Gomorrah, and the cities about them in like manner, giving themselves over to fornication, and going after strange flesh, are set forth for an example, suffering the vengeance of eternal fire."

It is better to enter into the Christian life maimed, that is deprived of some social advantage comparable to an eye, foot, or hand, than to keep all worldly advantages, and suffer the penalty of rejecting Christ, typified by fire, is the meaning of Matt. xviii:8; and Jude 7 teaches that Sodom and Gomorrah are an example of eternal fire. But that fire has expired. That the fire referred to is not endless is shown by the use of the term in the Bible. "God is a consuming fire," (Heb. xii:29,) but it is a "Refiner's fire." (Mal. iii:2-3.) It consumes the evil and refines away the dross of error and sin. This corroborates the meaning we have shown to belong to the word expressive of the fire's duration. But whatever may be the purpose of the fire, it is not endless, it is *aiónian*. Benson(68) well says: "The fire which consumed Sodom, &c., might be called eternal, as it burned till it had utterly consumed them, beyond the possibility of their being inhabited or rebuilt. But the word will have a yet more emphatical meaning, if (as several authors affirm) that fire continued to burn a long while."

EVERLASTING DESTRUCTION.

2 Thess. i:9. "Who shall be punished with *everlasting* destruction from the presence of the Lord, and from the glory of his power."

Everlasting destruction, *olethron aiónion*, does not signify remediless ruin, but long banishment from God's presence. This is what sin does for the soul. *Olethros* is not annihilation, but desolation. It is found but four times in the New Testament. 1 Thess. v:3, 1 Cor. v:5, 1 Tim. vi:9. The passage in 1 Cor. shows us how it is used: "deliver such a one unto Satan for the *destruction of the flesh, that the spirit may be saved in the day of the Lord Jesus.*" The destruction here is not final --it is conditional to the saving of the spirit. Everlasting destruction is equivalent to prolonged desolation.

THE BLACKNESS OF DARKNESS FOREVER.

2 Pet. ii:17. "These are wells without water, clouds that are carried with a tempest; to whom the mist of darkness is reserved forever." Jude 13. "Raging waves of the sea, foaming out their own shame; wandering stars, to whom is reserved the blackness of darkness forever." "To whom is always reserved the blackness of darkness," would be a correct paraphrase of this language. Those referred to are trees that bear no fruit, clouds that yield no water, foaming waves, stars that give no light. Endless duration was not thought of by either Peter or Jude. Indefinite duration, ages, is the utmost meaning of *eis aióna*, which is spurious in a 2 Peter ii:17, but genuine in Jude 13.

The literal meaning is, for an age. Eternity cannot be extorted from the phrase.

FOREVER AND EVER.

Heb. vi:2. "The doctrine of the aionian, (*aiónion*) judgment." We make no special explanation of this passage. Whether the judgment of that age or the age to come, the Christian is meant, matters not. "The judgement of the age" is the full force of the phrase aionion judgment. Rev. xiv:11. "And the smoke of their torment ascendeth up *forever and ever*: and they have no rest day nor night, who worship the beast and his image, and whosoever receiveth the mark of his name." xix:3. "And her smoke rose up *forever and ever*." xx:10. "And the devil that deceived them was cast into the lake of fire and brimstone, where the beast and the false prophet *are*, and shall be tormented day and night *forever and ever*."

Attempts have been made to show that these [are - editor] reduplications, if no other forms of the word convey the idea of eternity. But the literal meaning of *aiónas aiónon*, in the first text above, is ages of ages, and of *tous aiónas ton aiónon*, in the other two, is the ages of the ages. It is thus rendered in the Emphatic Diaglot. It is perfectly manifest to the commonest mind that if one age is limited, no number can be unlimited. Ages of ages is an intense expression of long duration, and if the word *aión* should be eternity, "eternities of eternities" ought to be the translation, an expression too absurd to require comment. If *aión* means eternity, any number of reduplications would weaken it. But while ages of ages is proper enough, eternity of eternities would be ridiculous. On this phraseology Sir Isaac Newton[(69)] says: "The ascending of the smoke of any burning thing *forever and ever*, is put for the continuation of a conquered people under the misery of perpetual subjection and slavery." The thought of eternal duration was not in the mind of Jesus or his apostles in any of these texts, but long duration, to be determined by the subject.

THE SPIRITS IN PRISON.

An illuminating side-light is thrown on this subject by commentators on 1 Pet. iii:18-20, in which Christ is said to have "preached unto the spirits in prison." Alford says our Lord "did preach salvation in fact, to the disembodied spirits, etc." Tayler Lewis

--[70] "There was a work of Christ in Hades, he makes proclamation '*ekeruxen*' in Hades to those who are there in ward. This interpretation, which was almost universally adopted by the early Christian church, etc." Professor Huidekoper.[71] "In the second and third centuries every branch and division of Christians believed that Christ preached to the departed." Dietelmair[72] says this doctrine "*in omni coetu Christiano creditum.*" Why preach salvation to souls whose doom was fixed for eternity? And how could Christians believe in that doctrine and at the same time give the aionian words the meaning of eternal duration?

AION MEANS AN EON, ÆON or AGE.

It is a pity that the noun (*aión*) has not always been rendered by the English word eon, or æon, and the adjective by eonian or aionion; then all confusion would have been avoided. Webster's Unabridged, defines it as meaning a space or period of time, an era, epoch, dispensation, or cycle, etc. He also gives it the sense of eternity, but no one could have misunderstood, had it been thus rendered. Suppose our translation read "What shall be the sign of thy coming, and of the end of the æon?" "The smoke of their torment shall ascend for æons of æons." "These shall go away into aionian chastisement, etc." The idea of eternity would not be found in the noun, nor of endless duration in the adjective, and the New Testament would be read as its authors intended.

Let the reader now recall the usage as we have presented it, and then reflect that all forms of the word are applied to punishment only fourteen times in the entire New Testament, and ask himself the question, Is it possible that so momentous a doctrine as this is only stated so small a number of times in divine revelation? If it has the sense of limited duration, this is consistent enough, for then it will be classed with the other terms that describe the Divine judgments. The fact that so many of those who speak or write never employ it at all, and that all of them together use it but fourteen times is a demonstration that He who has made known his will, and who would of all things have revealed so appalling a fate as endless woe, if he had it in preparation, has no such doom in store for immortal souls.

We now pass to corroborate these positions by consulting the views of those in the first centuries of the Christian Church, who obtained their opinions directly or indirectly from the apostles themselves.

5.--THE CHRISTIAN FATHERS.

Nothing can cast a backward illumination on the New Testament, and teach us the full meaning of our controverted words, as Jesus and the apostles used them, so well as the language of the Christian fathers and the early church. We will therefore consult those who were perfectly familiar with the Greek tongue, and who passed the word along down the ages, from the apostles to their successors, for more than five hundred years.

TAYLER LEWIS.

Prof. Tayler Lewis(73) in the course of learned disquisitions on the meaning of the Olamic and Aionian words of the Bible, refers to the oldest version of the New Testament, the Syriac, or the Peshito, and tells us how these words are rendered in this first form of the New Testament: "So is it ever in the old Syriac version where the one rendering is still more unmistakably clear. These shall go into the pain of the *Olam* (*aión*) (the world to come), and these to the life of the *Olam* (*aión*) (the world to come)." He refers to Matt. xix:16; Mark x: 17; Luke xviii:18; John iii:15; Acts xiii:46; 1 Tim. vi:12, in which *aiónios* is rendered *belonging to the olam*, or world to come.*Eternal life*, in our version, the words in Matt. xxv:46, are rendered in the Peshito "the life of the world to come."

We quote this not to endorse, but to show that one of the best of modern critics testifies that the earliest New Testament version did not employ endless as the meaning of the word. Of Prof. Lewis Dr. Beecher writes,(74) "We are not to suppose that so eminent an Orthodox divine says these things in support of Universalism, a system which he decidedly and earnestly rejects."

THE APOSTLES CREED.

The Apostles' Creed is the earliest Christian formula. The idea of endless torment is not hinted. "I believe in God, the Father Almighty; and in Jesus Christ, his only begotten Son, our Lord, who was born of the Virgin Mary by the Holy Ghost, was crucified under Pontius Pilate, buried, rose from the dead on the third day, ascended to the heavens, and sits on the right hand of the Father; whence he will come, to judge the living and the dead: and in the Holy Spirit; the holy church; the remission of sins; and the resurrection of the body."(75)

IGNATIUS.

Our first reference to the patristic writers shall be to Ignatius (A. D. 115) who says the reward of piety "is incorruptibility and eternal life," "love incorruptible and perpetual life." Here the aionian life is strengthened by incorruptible," showing that the word *aiónion* alone was in his mind unequal to the task of expressing endless duration. He says, also, that Jesus "was manifested to the ages" (*tois aiósin*). Of course he intended to use no such ridiculous expression as "to the eternities."

SIBYLLINE ORACLES.

The Sibylline Oracles --dated variously by different writers from 500 B. C., to 150 A. D., teach aionian suffering, and universal salvation beyond, showing how the word was then understood. The prophetess who professes to write the Oracles describes the saints as petitioning God for the salvation of the damned. Thus entreated she says "*God will deliver them* from the devouring fire and eternal gnashing of teeth."

JUSTIN MARTYR.

Justin Martyr, A. D., 140, 162, taught *everlasting* suffering, and annihilation afterwards. The wicked "are tormented as long as God wills that they should exist and be tormented. . . . . Souls both suffer punishment and die."(76) He uses the expression *aperanton aiona*.(77) "The wicked will be punished with *everlasting* punishment, and not for a thousand years as Plato asserted." Here punishment is announced as limited. This is evident from the fact that Justin Martyr taught the annihilation of the wicked; they are to be "tormented *world without end*," and then annihilated.

IRENÆUS.

Irenæus[78] says, "the unjust shall be sent into inextinguishable and *eternal* fire," and yet he taught that the wicked are to be annihilated: [79] "When it is necessary that the soul should no longer exist, the vital spirit leaves it, and the soul is no more, but returns thither whence it was taken." Dr. Beecher pertinently observes:[80] "What then are the facts as to Irenæus? Since he has been canonized as a saint, and since he stood in such close connection with Polycarp and with John the apostle, there has been a very great reluctance to admit the real facts of the case. Massuetus has employed much sophistry in endeavoring to hide them. Nevertheless, as we shall clearly show hereafter, they are incontrovertibly these: that he taught a final restitution of all things to unity and order by the annihilation of all the finally impenitent. Express statements of his in this creed, and in a fragment referred to by Prof. Schaff, on universal restoration,[81] and in other parts of his great work against the Gnostics, prove this beyond all possibility of refutation. The inference from this is plain. He did not understand *aiónios* in the sense of eternal; but in the sense claimed by Prof. Lewis, that is, pertaining to the world to come." These are his words: "Christ will do away with all evil, and make an end of all impurities." He further says[82] that certain persons "shall not receive from him (the Creator) length of days forever and ever." Thus the word denoted limited duration in his time, A. D. 170, 200.

HERMOGENES.

So Hermogenes (A. D. 200) who believed that all sinful beings will finally cease to be, must have understood Christ as applying *aiónion* to punishment in the sense of limited duration, or he would not have believed in annihilation, and have been a Christian.

ORIGEN AND THEODORE OF MOPSUESTIA.

Origen used the expressions "*everlasting* fire" and "*everlasting* punishment" to express his idea of the duration of punishment. Yet he believed that in all cases sin and suffering would cease and be followed by salvation. He was the most learned man of his time, and his example proves that *aiónion* did not mean endless at the time he wrote, A. D. 200 --253. Dr. Beecher says[83] "As an introduction to his system of theology, he states certain great facts as a creed believed by all the church. In these he states the doctrine of future retribution as *aiónion* life, and *aiónion* punishment, using the words of Christ. Now, if Origen understood *aiónion* as meaning strictly eternal, then to pursue such a course would involve him in gross and palpable self-contraction. But no one can hide the facts of the case. After setting forth the creed of the church as already stated, including *aiónion* punishment, he forthwith proceeds, with elaborate reasoning, again and again to prove the doctrine of universal restoration. The conclusion from these facts is obvious: Origen did not understand *aiónios* as meaning eternal, but rather as meaning pertaining to the world to come. . . . Two great facts stand out on the page of ecclesiastical history. One that the first system of Christian theology was composed and issued by Origen in the year 230 after Christ, of which a fundamental and essential element was the doctrine of the universal restoration of all fallen beings to their original holiness and union to God. The second is that after the lapse of a little more than three centuries, in the year 544, this doctrine was for the *first time condemned and anathematized* as heretical. This was done, not in the general council, but in a local council called by the Patriarch Mennos at Constantinople, by the order of Justinian. During all this long interval, the opinions of Origen and his various writings were an element of power in the whole Christian world. For a long time he stood high as the greatest luminary of the Christian world. He gave an impulse to the leading spirits of subsequent ages and was honored by them as their greatest benefactor. At last, after all his scholars were dead, in the remote age of Justinian, he was anathematized as a heretic of the worst kind. The same also was done with respect to Theodore of Mopsuestia, of the Antiochian school, who held the doctrine of universal restitution on a different basis. This, too, was done long after he was dead, in the year 553. From and after this point the doctrine of future eternal punishment reigned with undisputed sway during the middle ages that preceded the Reformation. What, then, was the state of facts as to the leading theological schools of the Christian world in the age of Origen and some centuries after? It was, in brief, this: There were at least six theological schools in the church at large. Of these six schools, one, and only one, was decidedly and earnestly in favor of the doctrine of future eternal punishment. One was in favor of the annihilation of the wicked. Two were in favor of the doctrine of universal restoration on the principles of Origen, and two in favor of universal restoration on the principles of Theodore of Mopsuestia.

"It is also true that the prominent defenders of the doctrine of universal restoration were decided believers in the divinity of Christ, in the trinity, in the incarnation and atonement, and in the great Christian doctrine of regeneration; and were, in piety, devotion, Christian activity and missionary enterprise, as well as in learning and intellectual power and attainments, inferior to none in the best ages of the church, and were greatly superior to those by whom, in after ages, they were condemned and anathematized.

"It is also true that the arguments by which they defended their views were never fairly stated and answered. Indeed, they were never stated at all. They may admit of a thorough answer and refutation, but even if so, they were not condemned and anathematized on any such grounds, but simply in obedience to the arbitrary mandates of Justinian, whose final arguments were deposition and banishment for those who refused to do his will.

"Consider, now, who Theodore of Mospuestia was, not as viewed by a slavish packed council, met to execute the will of a Byzantine despot, but by one of the most eminent evangelical scholars of Germany, Dorner. Of him he says: "Theodore of Mopsuestia was the crown and climax of the school of Antioch. The compass of his learning, his acuteness, and, as we must suppose, also, the force of his personal character, conjoined with his labors through many years, as a teacher both of churches and of young and talented disciples, and as a prolific writer, gained for him the title of Magister Orientis. He labored on uninterruptedly till his death in the year 427, and was regarded with an appreciation the more widely extended as he was the first Oriental theologian of this time."[84]

Mosheim says of Origen: "Origen possessed every excellence that can adorn the Christian character; uncommon piety from his very childhood; astonishing devotedness to that most holy religion which he professed; unequaled perseverence in labors and toils for the advancement of Christianity; and elevation of soul which placed him above all ordinary desires or fears; a most permanent contempt of wealth, honor, pleasures, and of death itself; the purest trust in the

Lord Jesus, for whose sake, when he was old and oppressed with ills of every kind, he patiently and perseveringly endured the severest sufferings. It is not strange, therefore, that he was held in so high estimation, both while he lived and after death. Certainly if any man deserves to stand first in the catalogue of saints and martyrs, and to be annually held up as an example to Christians, this is the man, for, except the apostles of Jesus Christ and their companions, I know of no one, among all those enrolled and honored as saints, who excelled him in virtue and holiness."(85)

How could universal salvation have been the prevailing doctrine in that age of the church unless the word applied to punishment in Matt. xxv:46 was understood by Christians to mean limited duration?

The fact that Origen and others taught an aionian punishment after death, and salvation beyond it, DEMONSTRATES *that in Origen's time the word had not the meaning of endless, but did mean at that date, indefinite or limited duration.*

Readers curious to look up this point of the state of opinion during the centuries following the age of Origen, can refer to the authorities cited below.(86)

EUSEBIUS.

Eusebius (A. D. 300-25) describes the darkness preceding creation thus:(87) "These for a long time had no limit," they continued "for a *long eternity*:" *dia polun aióna*. To say that darkness that *ended* with the creation endured for a long *eternity*, would be absurd.

GREGORY NYSSEN.

Gregory Nyssen (A. D. 370-3) proves that the word had the meaning of limited duration in his day. He says(88) "Whoever considers the divine power will plainly perceive that it is able at length to restore by means of the everlasting purgation and expiatory sufferings, those who have gone even to this extremity of wickedness." Thus everlasting punishment and salvation beyond was taught in the fourth century.

AUGUSTINE.

Augustine (A. D. 400-430) was the first known to argue that *aiónios* signified endless. He at first maintained that it always meant thus, but at length abandoned that ground, and only claimed that it had that meaning sometimes. He "was very imperfectly acquainted with the Greek language."(89)

AVITUS.

A. D. 410 Avitus brought to Spain, from Jerome, in Palestine, a translation of Origen, and taught that punishments are not endless; for "though they are called everlasting, yet that word in the original Greek does not, according to its etymology and frequent use, signify endless, but answers only to the duration of an age."(90)

GENERAL USAGE OF THE FATHERS.

In fact, every Universalist and every Annihilationist among the fathers of the early church is a standing witness testifying that the word was understood as we claim, in their day. Believers in the Bible, accepting its utterances implicitly as truth, how could they be Universalists or Annihilationists with the Greek Bible before them, and *aiónion* punishment taught there, unless they gave to the word thus used the meaning of limited duration? Accordingly, besides those alluded to above, we appeal to those ancient Universalists, the Basilidians (A. D. 130), the Carpocratians (A. D. 140), Clemens Alexandrinus (A. D. 190), Gregory Thaumaturgus (A. D. 220-50), Ambrose (A. D. 250), Titus of Bostra (A. D. 340-70), Didymus the Blind (A. D. 550-90), Diodore of Tarsus (A. D. 370-90), Isidore of Alexandria (A. D. 370-400), Jerome (A. D. 380-410), Palladius of Gallatia (A. D. 400), Theodore of Mopsuestia (A. D. 380-428), and others, not one of whom could have been a Universalist unless he ascribed to this word the sense of limited duration. To most of them Greek was as familiar as English is to us.

THE EMPEROR JUSTINIAN. The Emperor Justinian (A. D. 540), in calling the celebrated local council which assembled in 544, addressed his edict to Mennos, Patriarch of Constantinople, and elaborately argued against the doctrines he had determined should be condemned. He does not say, in defining the Catholic doctrine at that time "We believe in *aiónion* punishment," for that was just what the Universalist, Origen himself taught. Nor does he say, "The word*aiónion* has been misunderstood, it denotes endless duration," as he would have said had there been such a disagreement. But, writing in Greek with all the words of that copious speech from which to choose, he says, "The holy church of Christ teaches an endless *aiónios* (ATELEUTETOS*aiónios*) life to the righteous, and endless (*ateleutetos*) punishment to the wicked." *Aiónios* was not enough in his judgement to denote endless duration, and he employed *ateleutetos*. This demonstrates that even as late as A. D. 540 *aiónios* meant limited duration, and required an added word to impart to it the force of endless duration.

BELIEVERS IN ANNIHILATION AND IN UNIVERSAL SALVATION APPLIED THE WORD TO PUNISHMENT.

Thus Ignatius, Polycarp, Hermas, Justin Martyr, Irenæus, Hyppolytus, Justinian, and others, (from A. D. 115 to A. D. 544) use the word *aiónion* to define punishment. And yet, some of these taught that decay out of conscious existence is the natural destiny of men, from which some only are saved by God's grace. Previous to this decay or extinction of being, they held that men experience*aiónion* punishment. The *aiónion* punishment is not extinction of being, for that was the soul's natural destiny. The punishment is not endless for it ceases. Let us illustrate: Justin Martyr says "Souls suffer *aiónion* punishment and die." The punishment is in the future world, but it concludes with extinction, and yet it is *aiónion*. A. D. 540, *aiónion* required*ateleutetos* prefixed to convey the idea of endless duration.

OLYMPIODORUS.

Olympiodorus (sixth century) is quoted by Dr. Beecher[(91)] as saying, "When *aiónios* is used in reference to a period which, by assumption, is infinite and unbounded, it means *eternal*: but when used in reference to times or things limited, the sense is limited to them."

THE FIRST SIX CENTURIES.

Hence the word did not mean endless duration among the early Christians for about six centuries after Christ. To say that any one who contradicts these men is correct, and that they did not know the meaning of the word, is like saying that an Australian, twelve hundred years hence, will be better able to give an accurate definition of English words in common use to-day than we are ourselves. These ancients could not be mistaken, and the fact that they required qualifying words to give *aiónion* the sense of endless duration --that they used it to describe punishment when they believed in the annihilation of the wicked, or in their restoration subsequent to *aiónion* punishment, irrefragably demonstrates that the word had not the meaning of endless to them, and if not to them, then it must have been utterly destitute of it.

The uniform usage of these words by the early Church demonstrates that they signified temporal duration.

CONCLUSION.

Many sensible people will, with propriety, say, "Why all this labor to establish the meaning of one word?" And the author confesses that such a labor should be unnecessary. Men ought to refuse to credit such a doctrine as that of endless punishment on higher grounds than those of verbal definitions. Reverence, not to say respect, for God, the fact that he is the Father of mankind, should cause all to reject the doctrine of endless torment, though the weight of argument were a thousand fold to one in favor of the popular definition of this word. But there are many who disregard the moral argument against the doctrine, which is unanswerable; who crush under the noblest instincts of the heart and soul, which plead, trumpet-tongued, against that horrible nightmare of doubt and unbelief; who cling to the mere letter of the word which kills, and ignore the spirit which gives life; who insist that all the voices of reason and sentiment should be disregarded because the Bible declares the doctrine of endless punishment for sinners. It is for such that these facts have been gathered, and this essay written, that no shred nor vestige even of verbal probability should exist to mislead the mind, and so seem to sanction the doctrine that defames God and distresses man; that it might be seen that the letter and the spirit of the word agree, and are in perfect accord with the dictates of reason, the instincts of the heart, and the impulses of the soul, in rejecting the worst falsehood, the foulest of all brood of error, the darkest defamation of the dear God's character that ever yet was invented, the monstrous falsehood that represents him as consigning the souls he has created to his own image to interminable torment. The word under examination is the foundation stone of that evil structure.

Thus it has appeared as the result of this discussion that

1. There is nothing in the Etymology of the word warranting the erroneous view of it.

2. The definitions of Lexicographers uniformly given not only allow but compel the view we have advocated.

3. Greek writers before and at the time the Septuagint was made, always gave the word the sense of limited duration.

4. Such is the general usage in the Old Testament.

5. The Jewish Greek writers at the time of Christ ascribed to it limited duration.

6. The New Testament thus employs it.

7. The Christian Fathers for centuries after Christ thus understood it.

Hence it follows that the readers of the Bible are under the most imperative obligations to understand the word in all cases as denoting limited duration, unless the subject treated, or other qualifying words compel them to understand it differently. There is nothing in the Derivation, Lexicography or Usage of the word to warrant us in understanding it to convey the thought of endless duration.

If our positions are well taken the Bible does not teach the doctrine of endless torment, for it will be admitted that if this word does not teach it, it cannot be found in the Bible.

APPENDIX.

AIDIOS.

AN IMPORTANT WORD CONSIDERED.

There is but one Greek word beside *aiónios* rendered everlasting, and applied to punishment, in the New Testament, and that is the word *aidios* found in Jude 6: "And the angels which kept not their first estate, but left their own habitation, he hath reserved in *everlasting* chains under darkness unto the judgement of the great day." This word is found in but one other place in the New Testament, viz. Rom. i:20: "For the invisible things of him from the creation of the world are clearly seen, being understood by the things that are made, even his *eternal* power and Godhead."

Now it is admitted that this word among the Greeks had the sense of eternal, and should be understood as having that meaning wherever found, unless by express limitation it is shorn of its proper meaning. It is further admitted that had *aidios* occurred where *aiónios* does, there would be no escape from the conclusion that the New Testament teaches Endless Punishment. It is further admitted that the word is here used in the exact sense of *aiónios,* as is seen in the succeeding verse: "Even as Sodom and Gomorrah, and the cities about them in like manner, giving themselves over to fornication, and going after strange flesh, are set forth for an example, suffering the vengeance of *eternal* fire." That is to say, the "*aidios*" chains in verse 6 are "*even as*" durable as the *aiónion* fire" in verse 7. Which word modifies the other?

1. The construction of the language shows that the latter word limits the former. The *aidios* chains are even as the *aiónion* fire. As if one should say "I have been infinitely troubled, I have been vexed for an hour," or "He is an endless talker, he can talk five hours on a stretch." Now while "infinitely" and "endless" convey the sense of unlimited, they are both limited by what follows, as *aidios,* eternal, is limited by *aiónios,* indefinitely long.

2. That this is the correct exegesis is evident from still another limitation of the word. "The angels - - - he hath reserved in everlasting chains UNTO the judgement of the great day." Had Jude said that the angels are held in *aidios* chains, and stopped there, not limiting the word, we should not dare deny that he taught their eternal imprisonment. But when he limits the duration by *aiónion* and then expressly states that it is only *unto* a certain date, we understand that the imprisonment will terminate, even though we find applied to it a word that intrinsically signifies eternal duration, and that was used by the Greeks to convey the idea of eternity, and was attached to punishment by the Greek Jews of our Savior's times, to describe endless punishment, in which they were believers.

But observe, while this word *aidios* was in universal use among the Greek Jews of our Savior's day, to convey the idea of eternal duration, and was used by them to teach endless punishment, he never allowed himself to use it in connection with punishment, nor did any of his disciples but one, and he but once, and then carefully and expressly limited its meaning. Can demonstration go further than this to show that Jesus carefully avoided the phraseology by which his contemporaries described the doctrine of endless punishment? He never employed it. What ground then is there for saying that he adopted the language of his day on this subject? Their language was *aidios timoria*, endless torment. His language was *aionion kolasin*, age-lasting correction. They described unending ruin, he discipline, resulting in reformation.

1. Prideaux, Connection, Vol. III. Part ii. Book i.
2. "Etymologicum Linguæ Græcæ."
3. "Christian Examiner," Vol. X, p.42. He quotes the ancient Phavorinus as defining it thus: "The comprehension of many times or periods."
4. *De Cælo*, lib.i.cap.9.
5. Christian Union.
6. Chicago Tribune, quoted by Hon. C. H. Reed.
7. Christian Union. A series of remarkable papers was published in the Christian Union in 1873-4, by Edward Beecher, D. D., on the "History of Future Retribution."
8. Volume 2, pp. 500-550.
9. Theodoret, in Migne. Vol. IV, page 400.
10. Christian Examiner, Vol. X. page 47.
11. Christian Union.
12. Lange's Ecclesiastes.
13. Christian Examiner, Vols. x, xi, and xii. Boston: Gray & Bowen.
14. I. xxii, 58.
15. I. xxiv, 725.
16. Christian Union.
17. Theog 609.
18. Persæ 263.
19. Supp.572, cited by Prof. Tayler Lewis.
20. Nem. iii, 130.
21. Electra 1030.
22. De Mundo Cap.5.

23. In Metaph Lib. xiv.
24. Lib. ii.
25. Lib. i, Cap. 9.
26. Orestes, 596.
27. Ibid 971.
28. Med. 428.
29. Lib. viii cap 1.
30. De Repub. Lib. ii.
31. De Leg., Lib. x.
32. Timæus.
33. Cap. 5, p. 609 C.
34. Cap. 5, p. 610 A.
35. Metaph., Lib. xiv, cap. 7.
36. De Cælo., i, 9.
37. De Cælo, Lib. ii, cap. i.
38. Quoting from Timæus Locrus.
39. Ps. cslviii, 5, 6. Isa. xxx, 8 xxxiv, 10. Jer. vii, 7; xxv, 5.
40. 2 Sam. xii,10. Joel ii, 26, 27.
41. Univ. Book of Reference, pp. 106-7.
42. Gen. xvii, 7, 8, 13; xlviii, 4; xlix, 26. Ex. xl, 15. Lev. xvi, 34. Num. xxv, 13. Ps. xxiv, 7. Hab. iii, 6.
43. Deut. xv, 17. I Sam. i,22; xxvii, 12. Lev. xxv, 46. II Kings v, 27. Job xli, 4. I Kings i, 31. Neh. ii, 3. Dan. ii, 4. Exod. xiv, 13. Ecc. i,4. Ps. civ, 5; lxxviii, 69. Ezek. xxxvii, 25. Gen. xiii, 15. Exod. xxxii, 13. Josh. xiv, 9. I Chron. xxiii, 25. Jer. xvii, 25. Ps. xlviii, 8. Jer. xxxi, 40. I Kings viii, 13. Num. x,8; xviii, 24. I Chron. xxviii, 4. II Kings ix, 5. Josh. iv, 7. Jonah ii, 6. Ps. xxxvii, 29.
44. Gen. xvii:8; Ex. xl:15; xxi:6; Jonah ii:5,6.
45. Ex. xv:18; Dan. xii:3; Micah iv:5.
46. Note on Ecol. i:4, Lange's Com. pp. 45-50.
47. Second Inquiry.
48. Christian Union.
49. Hist. Jews vol. i: p. 117; Div. Leg. vol iii: pp. 1, 2 vol. v: Sermons xiii: Archæology p. 398; Essays, p.44.
50. Antiq. -- Wars.
51. Dr. Edward Beecher See p.17
52. See Griesbach, Knapp, and Wetstein.

53. Ex. Essays p.46.
54. Com. in loc.
55. Protag. Sec. 38, vol. 1, p. 252.
56. War. 3, 5, 8. Ant. 2, 4, 5, etc.
57. Theological Essays, Vol.1, pp. 143-162.
58. Sermons pp. 99-102.
59. Univ. Expositor, vol. 3, p. 446.
60. Univ. Expositor. vol. 3, p. 437.
61. Christian Examiner. Sept. 1830, pp. 25, 26.
62. Notes on Gal. i.
63. Burthog's "Christianity, a Revealed Mystery," pp. 17, 18. Note on Rom. xvi:25.
64. Notes on Matt. xii:31, 32.
65. Com. on loco.
66. Idem.
67. Paiges's Selections.
68. Paige Com. Vol. vi: p.398.
69. Daniel and Rev. London Ed. 1733, p. 18.
70. Lange on Eccl., 130.
71. Mission to the Underworld, pp. 51, 52.
72. Historia Dogmatis de Descensu Christi ad Inferos, chs. iv and vi.
73. Lange's Genesis, pp. 135, 144, and Ecclesiastes pp. 44, 51.
74. Christian Union.
75. Murdoch's Mosheim, vol. 1, p. 96.
76. Dialog. cum Tryphone pp. 222-3.
77. Apol. Prim cxxvii.
78. Adv. Her. p. v. cap. 27.
79. Ibid.
80. Christian Union.
81. Christian Union.
82. Schaff, vol. ii, pp. 504, 73.
83. Christian Union.
84. Doctrine of Person of Christ, Div. 2, vol. i, p. 50, Eninburgh.
85. Hist. Com. on Chris. before Constantine, vol. ii, p. 149.
86. Assemanni Bib. Orient. vol. iii, part i, pp. 223-4, 324.-Doderlein, Inst. Theol. Christ. vol. ii, pp. 200-1. -Jacobi, Bohn's Edition.-Neander's Hist. Christian Dogmas. -Guericke, Shedd's Translation.

pp. 308, 349. -Neander Torrey's Translation, vol. ii. p. 251-2. - Dorner's Hist. Person of Christ, 2 vol. pp. 28, 30, 50. - Dr. Schaff Hist. Christ Ch. vol. ii. pp. 731, 504. - Giesler, vol. i. p. 370. -Kurz, 1. Text Book Christ. Hist. p. 137-2:2. -Hagenbach, quoting from Augustine Civitate Dei, liber. xxi. chap. xvi.
NOTE. - Doderlein says: * The most learned in the early church, cherished and defended with most zeal the hope of a final cessation of torments. These are his words: Quanto quis altius eruditione in antiquitate Christianna eminuit, tanto magis spem finiendorum olim cruciatuum aluit atque defendit.
*Inst. Theol. Chris. vol. ii. p. 199.
87. History vol. i. p. 173.
88. De Infantibus, p. 173.
89. Ancient Hist. Univ.
90. Hieronymi Epist.
91. Christian Union.

Made in United States
North Haven, CT
13 January 2023

31030394R00046